THE FINANCE ACTS 1992

THE FINANCE ACTS 1992

A guide to the changes in taxation introduced by the two Finance Acts of 1992

ERNST & YOUNG

KOGAN PAGE

First published in 1992.

Kogan Page Limited
120 Pentonville Road
London N1 9JN

British Library Cataloguing in Publication Data
A CIP record for this book is available from the British Library.
ISBN 0 74 94 08 50 2

Printed and bound in Great Britain by Biddles Ltd,
Guildford and Kings Lynn

FOREWORD

Norman Lamont's Budget Speech of 10 March 1992 just preceded the general election, and only a small number of the measures he announced were enacted in the Finance Act 1992, which received Royal Assent on 16 March. The majority had to wait for the election and the Finance (No 2) Act, which received Royal Assent on 16 July 1992, and which also contained further measures announced in the meantime. All are contained in this guide to the Finance Acts 1992.

There are two major subjects covered which relate to the integration of tax within the European Community. Whilst harmonisation of tax regimes throughout Europe is some way distant, the greatest moves have taken place in the field of indirect tax, and we now see our VAT and Customs regimes significantly amended as a result of the abolition of fiscal frontiers and the creation of the Single Market. For the purposes of our text covering this, we are grateful for permission to use extracts from the commentary provided by HM Customs and Excise. Secondly, two EC directives in the field of direct taxation have led to corresponding UK legislation dealing with cross-border reorganisations and dividends respectively.

Other matters covered this year include the strengthening of legislation denying relief for corporate interest paid overseas, and against 'option arrangements' within groups of companies. These were introduced to counter cases lost by the Inland Revenue, but the legislation demonstrates an unnecessary degree of complexity and overkill.

Amongst other retrospective legislation is the Inland Revenue's third attempt at ensuring the collection of tax from transitional rules for building societies introduced in 1986, again in the face of taxpayer success in the courts.

On the other hand, relieving legislation granting further allowances for films, computer software and expensive cars is to be welcomed.

On the personal front, changes include the expansion of inheritance tax relief for business and agricultural property, and the introduction of the 'rent a room' scheme.

This book gives assistance in the interpretation of provisions which will inevitably make the tax aspects of our business lives more complex. The tax specialists at Ernst & Young have shared their understanding of the provisions as clearly and accurately as is possible without overburdening the reader with unnecessary detail. Rather than following the order of sections and schedules contained in the Acts, we have designed the book so that the reader should be able to find and understand most easily the subjects which interest him or her.

Whilst it is thus designed to be used by both taxpayers and their professional advisers, a book of this size cannot attempt to answer every question which arises in practice. It is recommended that specific advice is taken on any particular item before any action is taken.

Finally, I would like to thank the many partners and staff from the various specialist tax departments of Ernst & Young who have contributed their time and the benefits of their expertise to this publication. As a result, we hope readers will find this guide a most authoritative publication on the two Finance Acts of 1992 and, above all, of practical use both now and in the future.

Andrew Jones
National Tax Partner
Ernst & Young
July 1992

TABLE OF CONTENTS

Note: Section references are to the Finance (No 2) Act 1992 unless stated as Finance Act 1992 (FA92).

ABBREVIATIONS

ACT	Advance corporation tax
Board	Board of Inland Revenue
CAA	Capital Allowances Act 1990
CGT	Capital gains tax
CEMA	Customs and Excise Management Act
CGTA	Capital Gains Tax Act 1979
CP	Consultative Paper
CRT	Composite rate tax
CT	Corporation tax
Customs	Customs and Excise
DSS	Department of Social Security
EC	European Community
FA	Finance Act, for example FA91
FSA	Financial Services Act 1986
IHT	Inheritance tax
IRPR	Inland Revenue press release
IT	Income tax
NIC	National Insurance contribution
PEP	Personal equity plan
PRT	Petroleum revenue tax
Revenue	Inland Revenue
S	Section
SAYE	Save As You Earn
Sch	Schedule
SI	Statutory Instrument
SP	Statement of practice
TA	Income and Corporation Taxes Act 1988
TA70	Income and Corporation Taxes Act 1970
TCGA	Taxation of Chargeable Gains Act 1992
TMA	Taxes Management Act 1970
VAT	Value added tax
VATA	Value Added Tax Act 1983
VED	Vehicle excise duty

1.1 THE SINGLE MARKET

Technical changes are introduced consequent upon the abolition of fiscal frontiers from 1 January 1993 and the implementation of a new control regime for the commercial movement of goods subject to Excise duties.

S.1 This enables the Commissioners of Customs and Excise to make regulations fixing the time when excise duty is to be charged and the time when any infringement is deemed to have taken place. Introduces a new term 'the excise duty point', the time at which duty becomes payable.

The regulations, which will be made by SI, are also to determine person(s) liable for the duty.

Sch 1 The scope of the Customs and Excise Duties (General Reliefs) Act 1979 is extended. It includes new provisions to exempt goods from forfeiture for breach of the conditions of the relief, eg where an infringement is voluntarily disclosed and duty is paid. It also introduces penalties for non-compliance.

Minor amendments are also made to The Alcoholic Liquor Duties Act.

S.2 This enables the Commissioners to make new regulations for excise duty drawback where Customs are satisfied that goods have not been, and will not be, consumed in the UK, in view of the new arrangements for EC trade after 1992.

S.3 and Sch 2 These amend the Customs and Excise Management Act 1979 (CEMA) in relation to offences and penalties for the new excise duty arrangements.

New warehousing regulations will be introduced to regulate the deposit, keeping, securing and treatment of goods in a warehouse, to regulate the removal of goods and to enact new documentary requirements and controls.

The regulations will provide for the forfeiture of goods where there is non-compliance with the documentary controls. New penalties are introduced for non-compliance and Section 170 CEMA is amended to cover specific penalties for the evasion of excise duty.

The Schedule also includes an amendment to the Customs and Excise Duty (General Reliefs) Act 1979 to include forfeiture where goods are used in breach of the conditions for the relief.

Control of persons entering the UK S.4 and S.5

Various provisions of CEMA are amended to restrict Customs powers in relation to the control of persons and goods moving to and from other member states after 1992 except:

- where the movement is not in fact between member states
- to secure the collection of duty
- to enforce any EC prohibitions or restrictions that may still apply between the member states
- to enforce any UK prohibitions or restrictions that apply to imports and exports.

The legislation is also amended to enable baggage controls to take place at the airport of destination when persons enter the UK at one airport and take an internal flight to another, after 31 December 1992.

1.2 MOTOR VEHICLES

Vehicle Excise Duty
S.4 (FA92)

The rate of VED is increased by £10 for private cars, light goods vehicles and other vehicles previously licensed at £100 per annum. A reduced rate of £15 is also introduced for tricycles of 150cc or less. These changes relate to licences taken out after 10 March.

S.11 and S.12

The rates of Vehicle Excise Duty are amended for a number of farm vehicles. New legislation is also to be introduced to enable the removal of the exemption from VED for disabled persons which was introduced in Finance Act 1971.

Car tax and abolition of fiscal frontiers
S.18 and Sch 4

New regulations for the levying of car tax are to be introduced before 1 January 1993. Due to the abolition of Customs border controls for intra-Community movements, the Commissioners will make regulations for individuals and other non-registered persons to furnish particular documents to notify liability for car tax. The regulations will also include time limits for notification and payment. It should be noted that the time of acquisition of a vehicle is determined in accordance with VAT provisions.

The Car Tax Act 1983 is also amended to facilitate the new terminology, for example 'exported' is replaced by 'removed from the UK' and 'imported' is replaced by 'brought into the UK'.

Converted or imported vehicles
S.8 (FA92)

The rate of car tax on new converted or imported vehicles was reduced from 10% to 5% on 10 March.

1.3 MISCELLANEOUS

Changes in rates S.1, S.2, S.3 and Schedule (FA92) There are the usual increases in the rates of excise duty on alcoholic drinks, tobacco products and hydrocarbon oils, which took effect from 6pm on 10 March.

S.5 (FA92) The rate of General Betting Duty is reduced from 8% to 7.75% for bets placed in betting shops after 31 March.

S.6, S.17 The excise duty on matches and mechanical lighters is abolished from 1 January 1993. A large number of such imports come from other EC member states and collection of this duty after frontier controls are removed for EC goods would be very difficult. A further consequence is that matches become subject to VAT at the standard rate.

Bingo duty S.7 Members clubs will no longer have to pay bingo duty, or keep bingo records after 2 August 1992. This removes an onerous burden on small clubs.

Tobacco products S.8 Part of the excise duty charge on cigarettes is levied on their recommended retail price and the Tobacco Products Duty Act 1979 is amended to introduce a new definition of this. For goods of EC manufacture, it means any price recommended by the manufacturer and for manufacturers outside the EC, it means any price recommended by an importer.

Beer duty S.9 The Insolvency Act 1986 is amended to include beer duty as a preferential debt to Customs.

Search of aircraft S.10 Changes are made to CEMA in relation to Customs powers to stop and search aircraft.

2.1 PAYMENTS ON ACCOUNT

S.6 (FA92) Provision is made whereby the Treasury may make an order to the effect that registered businesses of a certain size shall have an obligation to make payments on account of their eventual liabilities at such times as may be determined.

In practice, this will result in large businesses (ie those with an annual net VAT liability in excess of £2m for the year to 31 March 1991) not having to submit monthly returns as originally proposed by the Government, but instead making monthly payments on account with a balancing payment at the time of submission of the quarterly returns. The first payments on account will be due in November 1992, December 1992, or January 1993 depending on the VAT quarters allocated to the business concerned.

The reason for this provision is that, as a result of the introduction of the Single Market provisions with effect from 1 January 1993, the Government would otherwise suffer a substantial shortfall in revenue, and is seeking to make good the deficit. Whilst it will be large businesses, as defined, which will be affected by these provisions, the shortfall in Government revenue arises as a result of changes affecting importers of goods from other member states, a different body of businesses, who are not necessarily 'large'.

2.2 MITIGATION OF PENALTIES

S. 7 (FA92) Two measures are introduced mitigating the VAT penalty regime:

- The serious misdeclaration penalty, originally fixed at 30% and subsequently reduced to 20%, is further reduced to 15% where the penalty is assessed after 10 March 1992, but does not apply in the case of a supplementary assessment if the original assessment had been made on or before 10 March 1992.
- The default surcharge is restricted to 20% in the case of fourth and subsequent defaults, relating to any liability to a surcharge arising on or after 1 April 1992.

2.3 THE SINGLE MARKET

S.14, Sch 3 This body of legislation seeks to implement the EC Directive which sets out the transitional VAT regime to apply to the abolition of fiscal frontiers from 1 January 1993. The date of implementation is to be fixed by reference to an order to be made by Customs.

Fundamental to the Single Market changes is the abolition of the concept of 'importation' of goods from a member state, and in its place the substitution of the concept of 'acquisition'. The overwhelming majority of the contents of Schedule 3 (which runs to more than 50 pages) relate to matters connected with the Single Market. Where the new legislation no more than reflects minor or consequential drafting changes, we have not given details here.

Basis of taxation
Para. 2 **Definition of the tax** – The definition of the tax is broadened to take account of acquisitions (formerly imports) of goods from other member states.

Goods will be regarded for VAT purposes as imported into the UK in the following circumstances:

- If they arrive in the UK from outside the EC, and are entered for own use in the UK;
- If they arrive in the UK from outside the EC, are entered to duty suspension arrangements – Customs and/or Excise warehousing, or free zone arrangements, or IPR suspension arrangements or temporary import arrangements – and subsequently leave those arrangements in the UK for home use; *or*
- If they arrive in the UK from outside the EC via another member state under a transit procedure, not having been put into free circulation in another member state, and at that time or subsequently are entered for home use in the UK.

Para. 3 **Scope of the tax** – The scope of the tax is extended so that it becomes chargeable on any taxable acquisition which takes place in the UK, where the acquisition is made by a taxable person, or the goods are subject to excise duty, or the goods are a new means of transport. Consequential amendments are made to the scope of the tax on imports, which by definition are confined to goods coming from places outside the member states.

Whilst the definition of a taxable person will remain unchanged, namely a person who is or who is liable to be registered, the legislative position relating to registration of necessity has become more complex; nonetheless, there will still be only a single register, and businesses will only be entitled to be registered once.

Para. 4 **Meaning of 'supply'** – The legislation is to be amended so that the transfer by a taxable person of goods from one member state to another for the purpose of his business there shall be treated as a supply of goods. However, it is intended that this provision should not apply in certain circumstances such as:

- The transfer of goods to another member state in pursuance of a supply which is deemed to take place in the other member state (installed or assembled goods or distance sales);
- The transfer of goods to another member state where process or repair work (whether a supply of goods or services) is to be carried out on the goods before return to the UK;
- The temporary use of the goods in the member state to which they are transferred by the person who transfers them, in order to make a supply of services in that member state, etc.

Paras. 5 and 6 **Time of supply** – A new time of supply provision is to be introduced by regulation, applying solely to the supply of goods zero-rated in the UK for acquisition by a registered business in another member state.

The time of supply in this case will be the earlier of:

- The fifteenth day of the month following that in which the basic tax point occurs; *or*
- The date of issue of a tax or other prescribed invoice in respect of the supply.

The time of supply of goods made in the UK to unregistered customers in another member state (which will be taxed in the UK) will be determined in accordance with the normal domestic time of supply rules.

Para. 7 **Place of supply** – The existing legislation in Section 6 VATA provides tests for determining whether goods or services are supplied in the United

Kingdom. The main amendments are as follows:

Installed and assembled goods are deemed to be supplied in the United Kingdom where their supply involves their installation or assembly at a place in the United Kingdom to which they are removed.

Where an overseas business is, or is liable to be, registered in the UK by virtue of distance sales in the UK, or would be so liable were it not registerable under other provisions, the place of supply of any supplies of goods made to an unregistered UK customer, where the supplier arranges the transportation of the goods, will be the UK. Conversely, where a UK-based business is making distance sales in another member state, and is, or is liable to be, registered and account for VAT in that member state, the place of supply of his supplies to his unregistered customers will be outside the UK, and in that other member state. These provisions do not apply in the case of persons supplying goods, other than excise duty goods, by distance selling under the relevant threshold prescribed by each member state. In the UK this threshold has been set at £70,000.

Where goods are imported into the UK, in the course of a supply, and the supplier is the person by whom, or under whose directions, they are imported, the goods will be treated as being supplied in the UK. Further, goods shall be treated as supplied in the UK where they are despatched from the UK when they are supplied, and as supplied outside the UK in any other case.

Para. 8 **Reverse charges** – The reverse charge legislation is to be amended to enable the taxation of intra-EC freight transport and associated services supplied to a taxable person belonging in another member state.

Para. 10 **Acquisition of goods**

(a) *Meaning of 'acquisition'*. The acquisition of goods from another member state is any acquisition of goods in pursuance of a transaction where both of the following conditions are satisfied:

- the transaction is, or is treated for the purposes of the Act, as a supply of goods; *and*
- the transaction involves the removal of the goods from another member state.

It does not matter whether the transport of the goods is undertaken by or on behalf of the supplier, or by or on behalf of the customer.

The legislation also provides that the transfer of a person's own goods to another member state is an acquisition of goods in that member state. However, power is also given to the Treasury to provide by order that any acquisition of any goods shall not be treated as such in prescribed circumstances.

(b) *Time of acquisition*. Tax on acquisition shall become due at the time of acquisition, which will be the earlier of:

- The fifteenth day of the month following that in which the first relevant event occurred; *and*
- The date of issue of an invoice by the supplier.

The 'first relevant event' is defined as:

- The date of first removal of the goods (ie if the goods had been supplied in the UK, the basic tax point determined in accordance with the existing legislation); *or*
- In the case of sale or return goods, the time when it becomes certain that the goods have been acquired, or twelve months after the date of first removal, if sooner.

In most cases the date of issue of an invoice is likely to be the relevant test. It should be noted that there is no payment tax point for acquisitions.

(c) *Place of acquisition*. An acquisition will be taxable in the member state in which it takes place. The basic rule is that goods will be acquired in the UK if the transport of the goods ends in the UK, the goods having been despatched either from another member state, or from a third country but transiting through another member state.

Goods will also be treated as acquired in the UK where a person uses a UK VAT registration number in order to acquire goods, whether or not the goods are to be transported to the UK. If the goods are not to be received by the acquirer in the UK, but are delivered to another member state, there will also be an acquisition in that other member state under the corresponding provisions applicable there.

Power is given to Customs to make regulations which will provide that:

- Where it is established in accordance with the regulations that

VAT has been paid in another member state on the acquisition of the goods in accordance with the corresponding provisions applicable there, the goods will not be treated as acquired in the UK;

- Where VAT is paid both in the UK and in another member state under the corresponding provisions applicable there (the goods having been delivered to that other member state), then the VAT paid in the UK will be refunded provided input tax has not already been credited in respect of the acquisition in the UK.

Paras. 15 and 16 **Credit of tax on acquisition against output tax** – The existing definition of 'input tax' is to be extended to include tax on the acquisition of any goods in the UK. The effect of the changes is to provide for payment of tax on acquisitions made by a taxable person in the UK to be accounted for and paid in line with the existing arrangements for domestic supplies (ie the normal VAT return). In consequence the right is given to input tax deduction on the VAT paid on acquisition of goods, subject to the normal rules.

Additionally, the right to deduction is extended to cover the cases of supplies outside the United Kingdom, and such exempt supplies as the Treasury may by order specify. This power will be used to restore the right to deduction in the case of supplies of services previously supplied zero-rated in the UK, but which under the new place of supply provisions for services will be treated as made outside the United Kingdom, or which are made and exempt in the United Kingdom.

Para. 35 **Supplies of dutiable goods in warehouse** – The treatment of supplies of third country goods and of UK-produced goods in warehouse will be unchanged, but amendments to the legislation deal with acquisitions from other member states of goods under warehousing arrangements. This is done by the mechanism treating the acquisitions (and supplies) as taking place outside the UK. As at present, full records of any transactions in warehouse must be kept.

In free zones, the current arrangements for payment of import VAT will remain for goods from third countries. The treatment of supplies of free zone goods will be unchanged.

Acquisitions of goods from other member states will be dealt with similarly to acquisitions outside free zones. These principles will also apply to supplies and acquisitions of goods under other duty suspension arrangements.

Para. 44 **Taxation under the law of other member states** – Provision is made to recognise that in some cases, a person's obligations in the UK may depend on the legislation in place in another member state and to allow Customs to fulfil their obligations under the requirements of the EC Regulation on administrative co-operation.

Territories included in references to other member states – New legislation gives Customs powers to make regulations prescribing special territories (eg the Canary Islands) which are treated for customs purposes as if they were part of the EC, to be treated for VAT purposes as if they were outside the EC. Customs legislation is applied to goods moving between those territories and the UK, as if the goods were entering or leaving the UK from outside the EC.

Para. 45 **Meaning of 'new means of transport'** – This provision defines those motor vehicles, boats and aircraft which are always to be subject to taxation in the member state of destination. The criteria reflect those laid down in the amendment Directive and are based on technical specifications (length, engine size, etc) and a definition of 'new'. Regulations made under this provision will lay down the detailed rules for determining the meaning of 'first entry into service' which defines when VAT is due.

Para. 59 **Distance selling** – A new Schedule 1A, VATA, is introduced dealing with the registration requirements in respect of the new 'distance selling' arrangements. All sales to non-taxable persons in another member state where the supplier takes responsibility for the delivery of the goods will be taxed in the member state of the destination once the value of those sales to that member state exceeds an annual threshold or where the supplier opts to be treated in this way. This threshold has been set at 100,000 ECU (£70,000) but member states have the option to set a lower threshold of 35,000 ECU. Once the threshold has been exceeded, the place of supply of any further distance sales will be the member state of destination, and the supplier will thus be liable to register, or appoint a tax representative there, to account for the tax due.

The threshold to be applied for distance selling in the UK will be £70,000; businesses which make distance sales to non-taxable persons in the UK in excess of this threshold will be liable to register and account for tax in the UK. Unlike the provisions of the existing Schedule 1, the threshold is calculated on the sales made in the current year from 1 January to date. The effective date of registration will be the date of the first relevant supply (as defined) after the threshold has been breached.

Distance sales of excisable goods are always taxable in the member state of destination; traders making such sales are therefore liable to be registered from the time of the first relevant supply. Conversely, supplies of new means of transport can never be distance sales. Distance sellers are therefore to exclude sales of both goods subject to excise duty and new means of transport when calculating the level of distance sales for the purposes of the threshold.

Persons with no place of business in the UK may be required to appoint a tax representative who will be responsible for accounting for and paying tax in the UK.

Distance sellers whose sales to the UK do not exceed £70,000 will be entitled to opt to have their supplies treated as though they were taxable here. This option is exercised in their own member state, and must remain in force for a minimum of two calendar years. This option would be valuable where, for example, the relevant rate of VAT in the United Kingdom was less than in the other member state. Once the option has been exercised, the business becomes liable to be registered under this Schedule 1A, and the effective date of registration will be the date of the first relevant supply following the exercise of the option.

Provision is made for businesses to request registration before the option has been exercised – subject to conditions laid down by Customs, as with the existing rules relating to intending traders.

Once registered, a person's registration will only be cancelled when he ceases to be liable to be registered under all Schedules, or has been registered for at least two calendar years if registered by virtue of the exercise of an option.

Regulations will be made which extend the existing regulations to include persons registered under Schedule 1A; require notification of liability to be registered to be made on a specified form; and require registered persons to issue tax invoices to all their customers, including private individuals.

Registration in respect of acquisitions from other member states – Schedule 1B will introduce the provisions for the registration of any body or person (other than a private individual who is not in business) who acquires goods from other member states in excess of the new acquisition threshold but who is not currently registered, or required to be registered, under either existing Schedule 1 or new Schedule 1A (see above).

This threshold will be set initially at the same level as the current Schedule 1 threshold, ie £36,600, but as with Schedule 1A, will be based on the current year from 1 January to date. Additionally, any person who expects to acquire goods of a value exceeding £36,600 in the ensuing 30 days will be liable to register. Acquisitions of excisable goods and new means of transport are always taxable in the member state of destination and are therefore to be excluded when calculating whether a person's acquisitions have breached the threshold.

While a person is below the threshold, and is not otherwise registered for VAT, tax on the acquisitions he makes, and which he must count towards the threshold, will be charged on his supply at the rate in force in the member state where the goods are supplied. Once he is registered under Schedule 1B, he will account for the tax on his acquisitions in the UK subject to the normal rules.

As with Schedule 1A, there is to be an entitlement to register voluntarily. Those persons registering voluntarily will have to remain registered for at least two calendar years, although persons who are not registered or liable to be registered under either Schedule 1 or 1A, and who only makes acquisitions of excisable goods, will not be entitled to register under Schedule 1B.

Where a person makes acquisitions and is able to satisfy Customs that any such acquisitions would be zero-rated if he were registered under these provisions, then he may be exempted from registration.

Once registered, the registration will only be cancelled when the business ceases to be liable to be registered under all Schedules, or it has been registered for at least two calendar years if registered voluntarily.

Regulations will be made which extend the existing regulations to include persons registered under Schedule 1B, requiring notification of liability to be registered to be made on a specified form.

Para. 60 **Transfers of goods between branches** – A person is deemed to be making a supply of goods if he removes goods forming part of the assets of his business from one member state to another in the course or furtherance of his business. However, there are two exceptions:

- If the goods are removed from one part of a member state to another.
- If the goods are removed from a place outside the member state to one within, via a second member state, without being put into free circulation in that second member state.

Rates and valuation
Para. 11 **Rate of tax** – The existing legislation is amended to provide that the standard rate of tax will be charged on the acquisition of goods in the UK, by reference to the value of acquisition of goods acquired. It follows that any goods, the supply of which would be exempt or zero-rated in the UK, will give rise to an exempt or zero-rated acquisition respectively.

Para. 12 **Value of supply of goods and services** – Following a decision of the European Court of Justice, the legislation relating to valuation is amended in circumstances where the consideration for a supply does not consist, or does not wholly consist, of money. Instead of the value being taken as its open market value, it is such amount in money as, with the addition of the tax chargeable, is equivalent to the consideration. As well as affecting the amount of VAT due on barter and exchange transactions, the change will help clarify the treatment of many business promotion schemes.

Para. 13 **Valuation of acquisitions** – The existing legislation is to be amended so that the valuation of acquisitions of goods should be on the same basis as for the domestic supply of equivalent goods.

Para. 14 **Valuation of importations (from places outside the member states)** – The existing legislation is amended to provide that the Customs rules be used for import VAT valuation purposes.

Para. 61 **Valuation** – The power of Customs to direct valuations of imported goods at open market value is repealed.

The value of a supply for VAT purposes includes excise duty, car tax, EC Customs duty and/or agricultural levies chargeable on importation if the supply involves removal of goods to the UK. An important amendment enables VAT registered businesses to make donations of goods or assets to third parties and account for output tax by reference to the current value of assets, rather than historical cost as hitherto. This will be of particular benefit to businesses wishing to donate unused obsolete computer equipment to educational establishments. Where services are imported under the reverse charge provisions, in a case where the consideration for which the services were in fact supplied was a consideration in money, the value is such amount as is equal to that consideration; and in a case where the consideration did not consist or not wholly consist of money, the value is such amount in money as is equivalent to that consideration.

Where goods or services are supplied, and invoiced in a foreign currency, the value for VAT will continue to be calculated by reference to the Customs period exchange rate. In the case of acquisitions and domestic supplies, businesses will, in practice, be able to choose between the latest market selling rate, the Customs period exchange rate, or their own commercial rate (subject to approval by their local VAT office).

Para. 62 **Valuation of acquisitions from other member states (special cases)** – The existing provisions relating to transactions between connected persons are extended to acquisitions; Customs may direct that the value of an acquisition will be its open market value, where the supplier and the customer are connected and the customer is partly or wholly exempt. Provision is made in para. 40 (see below) for appeals to be lodged against such directions.

Power is given to Customs to make regulations prescribing the inclusion of any excise duty or car tax chargeable on an acquisition of goods to be included in the taxable amount for VAT.

Appropriate provision is made for valuations of acquisitions by reference to the current purchase price of identical or similar goods, or the current production cost of the goods. Any VAT included in the purchase price or production is to be deducted in arriving at the value to be taxed.

Reliefs and exemptions

Para. 17 **Zero-rating relief** – This paragraph gives the statutory authority (as noted above) for the zero-rating of acquired goods, where the supply of equivalent goods in the UK would have been zero-rated. This paragraph is also the authority for the zero-rating of supplies to registered persons (ie acquirers) in other member states. Regulations will provide that the supply of goods removed from the UK to another member state can be zero-rated provided the supplier can demonstrate that the goods have been supplied to the customer with a valid registration number of another member state; that the goods have left the UK, and that such other conditions as may be specified in regulations made by Customs are fulfilled. The existing Regulation relating to retail export schemes will be amended to restrict their application to persons travelling to a destination outside the EC.

Provision is made for Regulations to zero-rate supplies in duty and tax-free shops to intra-EC travellers. Inter alia, these will specify the limits involved, set conditions, and allow VAT to be charged on purchases over the value of quantity limits.

Para. 18 **Exemptions** – Provision is made to ensure that an acquisition of goods from another member state is an exempt acquisition, if the equivalent supply in the UK would also have been exempt.

Para. 19 **Relief on supply of certain second-hand goods** – The existing legislation relating to imports is amended so that the relief applies just as much to future acquisitions from member states, as it does to importations from outside the Single Market.

Para. 20 **Relief from tax on importation of goods** – The existing legislation is amended to restrict its scope to goods imported from outside the EC (as opposed to acquisitions from other member states). New regulations will provide relief from VAT on the importation of goods where the goods arrive in the UK from outside the EC, and are supplied under the zero-rating provisions by the UK importer for acquisition by a registered person in another member state.

Refunds
Para. 21 **Refunds of tax** – The legislation relating to refunds of tax to local authorities who make acquisitions from other member states is amended to take account of the Single Market, to include VAT on EC acquisitions.

Para. 22 **Refunds of tax relating to new means of transport** – Provision is made for an entitlement for a non-registered person to obtain a refund of tax in certain circumstances where he supplies a new means of transport to a person in another member state.

Para. 23 **Do-it-yourself builders** – Provision is made to ensure refunds in respect of acquisition tax paid in the UK by do-it-yourself builders in the prescribed circumstances, and, in order to prevent discrimination against non-registered persons including private individuals, a corresponding right to refund is given in respect of any VAT charged on the relevant goods by a supplier in another member state.

Agents and representatives
Para. 33 **Agents, etc** – The existing provision whereby Customs may direct that any agent, manager or factor who is resident in the United Kingdom should be accountable for VAT on behalf of a person not resident in the United Kingdom, is repealed. The existing legislation is modified so that an agent who is registered for VAT in the UK may account for VAT on the acquisition by his unregistered principal of goods in the UK, deduct that tax as input tax (subject to the normal rules), but must also account for any output tax on the subsequent supply of those goods.

Para. 34 **Tax representatives** – A new provision is made whereby Customs may require a person who is, or is liable to be, registered in the UK or who is otherwise making taxable supplies or acquisitions in the UK, and who is established overseas, with no place of business in the UK, to appoint a tax representative in the UK. The tax representative will be responsible for accounting for VAT on his principal's behalf and will have a joint and several liability for compliance in all matters which could otherwise be the sole responsibility of the principal. This provision extends beyond EC residents to encompass any overseas resident who is a taxable person in the UK.

If an overseas resident fails to appoint a tax representative when directed to do so, Customs will be able to require security to be provided to cover payment of tax due. Where any such security has been required, and is not lodged, it will be recoverable as if it were tax, and there may be a liability to a criminal penalty.

Regulations will be made to lay down the way in which a tax representative is to be appointed, and Customs notified. The regulations will also set out the circumstances in which a person will cease to be treated as a tax representative.

Additionally, in a new provision which is relevant both to 'triangulation' and 'supply and install' contracts under the Single Market regime the recipients of supplies are to be permitted to account for and pay any tax on the supply of goods, on behalf of the supplier, so avoiding the need for an overseas supplier to register and account for VAT. 'Triangulation' is the name given to the situation in which a company in one member state invoices some goods to a company or trader in another member state for delivery to a third trader in a third member state.

This provision applies if the supplier:

- does not have any business establishment or other establishment in the UK and does not have his usual place of residence in the UK;
- is for the time being neither registered nor required to be registered for VAT;
- does not have a tax representative and is not for the time being required to appoint one; *and*
- intends that his taxable supplies should be confined to supplies of goods made to taxable persons who are willing to account for and pay the tax chargeable thereon.

It is provided that the taxable person in receipt of the supply should give (and not withdraw) an undertaking to account for any tax chargeable on supplies of goods made to him by the supplier in question, and Customs may by regulation provide for:

- the form and manner in which tax should be accounted for, or any undertaking should be made or withdrawn;
- the manner in which the making or withdrawal of any such undertaking should be notified to Customs;
- a person whose taxable supplies for the time being fall to be taxed in accordance with this section to be under an obligation to notify Customs if he makes any taxable supplies to which this provision does not apply, and which are not zero-rated; *and*
- prescribed provisions of the VAT legislation to have effect, whereunder a person supplied with any goods is required to account for and pay any tax on the supply, as if that tax were on supplies or acquisitions made by him.

Penalties and administration
Para. 39

Offences and penalties – Regulations are to be introduced to apply penalties to fraudulent or incorrect refunds obtained under other legislation introduced under the Single Market regime. A supplier in another member state who is required to be registered because of his distance sales to the UK, may be required to appoint a tax representative when he has no place of business in the UK. This also applies to any other overseas person who has no place of business in the UK but is registered for VAT.

Where such a person fails to appoint a tax representative, Customs may require security, and failure to do so will be an offence. Currently Customs take action to stop a registered business trading where a requested security has not been provided, but this will not be the case where a tax representative has not been appointed.

Para. 40

Appeals – The legislation has been extended to allow a right of appeal against:

- Tax chargeable on acquisition.
- The amount of any refund due under new provisions in this Act.
- Any direction made by Customs concerning the value of an acquisition.
- An assessment of tax due from an unregistered person on the acquisition of goods subject to excise duty, or of a new means of transport.

- A requirement to provide security where a person fails to appoint a tax representative.

- The new penalties imposed in relation to new means of transport, exempt bodies, distance selling, and EC sales statements.

Para. 51 **Cessation of liability to be registered** – Legislation makes it clear that a person cannot cease to be liable to be registered until such time as he has in fact been registered.

Para. 64 **Administration, collection and enforcement** – The existing legislation relating to invoices is confined to 'tax invoices' issued to taxable persons. The new provisions will require the issue of invoices, containing specified information, for zero-rated supplies, supplies to non-taxable persons, etc. Customs indicate that regulations to be made under these new provisions will require:

- invoices to be issued to non-taxable persons;

- an invoice containing specified information to be issued where a zero-rated supply is made;

- the VAT number of the customer in another member state to be shown on tax invoices where the goods are supplied free of tax;

- taxable persons to provide tax invoices in respect of any payment on account made to them; *and*

- invoices to show details of size, age and usage for supplies of new means of transport.

Customs will also have the power to allow invoices from suppliers in other member states to be treated as if they were tax invoices, notwithstanding that the documents may not otherwise conform to UK legislation.

Power is given to Customs to require the submission of EC sales statements (otherwise known as aggregate sales lists) by all VAT registered businesses making supplies to VAT registered traders in other member states.

Regulations to be made under these provisions will require submission of EC sales statements by UK registered businesses who:

- make supplies of goods to a taxable person in another member state;

- send goods to another member state for process;
- return goods to another member state after processing; *or*
- transfer their own goods to another member state.

The regulations will require an EC sales statement completed by or on behalf of a UK registered person to contain the following information:

- his own VAT registration number;
- the VAT registered number of his customer in another member state, together with a country identifier; *and*
- the aggregate value of goods and associated services supplied to that customer.

Where goods are sent for processing, the relevant EC sales statements must show:

- when goods are sent for processing, an indication that goods have been transferred for processing (but no value for the goods is shown); *and*
- when the goods are returned after processing, the value of the process work which has taken place, and an indication that the goods are being returned after processing.

Statements will normally be required to be submitted on a calendar quarter basis. However, Customs may allow more frequent submission. Statements must reach Customs within six weeks from the end of the period. Nil returns will not be required. Statements will need to be signed by the taxable person or his representative to the effect that the list is true and complete.

Customs will allow those UK businesses who use non-standard accounting periods to submit their EC sales statements using these accounting periods, provided they are in general agreement with calendar quarters.

The regulations will allow submission of an EC sales statement in one of the following forms:

a) a pre-printed return provided by Customs;

b) a plain paper return produced by computer;

c) magnetic media; *or*

d) electronic data exchange.

(b), (c) and (d) will need prior approval from Customs in order to agree content, layout and computer compatibility.

A registered person who is required to submit an EC sales statement will be required to keep records showing how the statement is made up. He will also be required to keep an EC sales (summary) account similar to the VAT account.

New provisions enable Customs to make regulations concerning the control of acquisitions of new means of transport and goods subject to excise by non-taxable persons. Basically, acquisitions (other than distance sales) of excisable goods by non-registered persons, and all acquisitions of new means of transport, are to be taxed in the member state of destination.

In order to avoid the need to register all persons making such acquisitions (who would not otherwise be liable to be registered) a different mechanism will operate to collect the VAT due. Regulations made under these provisions will require non-registered persons acquiring such goods to notify Customs of their liability to pay VAT on their acquisitions of new means of transport and goods subject to excise duty. The regulations will lay down the time limits for such notification, and the information that is to be given in any notification. The amount of tax due will be assessed by Customs on the basis of the information provided in the notification. The regulations will also provide for how the tax is to be paid.

Para. 74 **Evidence by certificate** – Failure to submit an EC sales statement, or to notify an acquisition, is proved by a certificate to be furnished by Customs.

Para. 79 **Inaccuracies in EC sales statements** – Provision is made for penalties in respect of EC sales statements which are found to be inaccurate. Initially, the provisions will allow a warning letter to be issued for the first 'material inaccuracy', but the submission of further inaccurate statements within two years of the warning letter will result in the issue of a 'Notice of Liability to Penalty', and the taxable person will then be liable to a penalty of £100 for each inaccurate statement submitted within two years of the issue of the notice.

An EC sales statement will be regarded as inaccurate if it includes information which it should not contain, omits information which it should contain or is misleading in any material respect. Customs indicate that they will not normally penalise persons for minor inaccuracies on EC sales statements.

The penalty provisions will not apply if Customs are satisfied that there was a reasonable excuse for the inaccuracy. There will also be a right of appeal to a VAT tribunal.

Paras. 80 and 81 **Penalties for breach of regulatory provisions** – Persons who are liable to be registered under the new registration provisions will be subject to civil penalty if they fail to register for VAT at the proper time. The penalty will be based on a percentage of the relevant tax with a minimum of £50. This is in line with a present penalty applicable to failure to register, but the amount of tax which is used as the basis of the penalty will be adjusted to take account of tax paid either to a supplier in another member state or directly to the fiscal authority of that member state (for example, by a distant seller). This adjustment will also apply when a person fails to register under the present Schedule 1, but has made acquisitions on which tax must be declared on a UK VAT return.

Further, the penalty provisions are extended to cover circumstances where a registered person fails to notify the end of liability or entitlement to be registered, or fails to notify any other significant change as required under the regulations.

Para. 82 **Penalties for failure to submit EC sales statements** – New provisions impose penalties for taxable persons who breach the regulations requiring the submission of EC sales statements.

The main provisions are for notification to the taxable person of the default in relation to the EC sales statement specified and forewarning that any further defaults within a period of twelve months will be liable to a penalty.

If further defaults occur a penalty will be applied in respect of the length of time for which the default continues up to a maximum of 100 days. The penalty will be £5 per day for the first default, £10 for the second and £15 for the third. The maximum penalty is £15 per day.

The penalty will not apply if Customs are satisfied there was reasonable excuse for the failure, and there will be a right of appeal to a VAT tribunal against the application of the penalty.

Para. 83 **Interest** – Interest is to be charged where tax has been assessed on acquisitions by a taxable person who had been incorrectly exempted from registration.

Paras. 84 and 85 **Penalty framework** – Provision is made to ensure that the new penalty framework relating to penalties under the Single Market regime are treated in like manner to penalties relating to non-compliance with the existing domestic regime.

2.4 REPAYMENT SUPPLEMENT

S. 15 Following a defeat in the Courts, the Government is seeking to amend the legislation relating to repayment supplement, and interest in certain cases of official error.

In both cases, there is with effect from Royal Assent to be a new definition of the period for raising and answering enquiries relating to claims for either repayment supplement or interest, so that the period should commence with the date on which Customs first consider it necessary to make such an enquiry; and should end with the date on which Customs either satisfy themselves that they have received a complete answer to the enquiry, or determine not to make the enquiry or, if they have made it, not to pursue it further.

2.5 FARMERS

Flat rate farmers schemes S.16

A new provision will for the first time enable farmers to benefit from the VAT regime without being registered; this will bring the United Kingdom legislation in line with that of the other member states, except Denmark.

The basic mechanics of the scheme are that those eligible to be treated as flat rate farmers are entitled to be compensated for the VAT charged on their expenditure by adding a fixed percentage to the amount of their supplies of agricultural products and services, which the recipient of the supply in question is able to deduct if he is a registered taxable person. The fixed percentage added to the price is not however VAT, and the flat rate farmer does not have to register under the normal VAT system.

The fixed percentage, instead of being the standard rate or zero rate, will be a fixed rate applicable to all agricultural products and services, whatever their liability. The percentage will be fixed by regulation, but it is likely to be in the range from 3% to 6%, since this is thought to be approximately what is needed to compensate a person for the VAT on his expenditure in the agricultural sector.

Under the UK scheme, Customs are proposing that there should be no threshold for eligibility; farmers of whatever size will be able to make a choice between registering under the normal VAT system, or coming within the flat rate compensation scheme. However, this is only where their outputs are agricultural in nature, as defined. Where farmers engage in other activities such as running camp sites or golf clubs, they will have to register under the normal system once the turnover exceeds the registration threshold, in which event they would no longer be eligible for the flat rate compensation scheme.

2.6 MOTOR VEHICLES

The Value Added Tax (Cars) (Amendment) Order 1992

This order, which is effective from 1 August 1992, enables private taxi firms, self-drive hire firms, and driving schools to reclaim the tax on purchases of motor cars for their businesses (where registered). It ensures that tax is charged on the full selling price of these cars when sold by those businesses in their turn; and also creates a self-supply of the motor car where an input deduction has been taken, and the car is put to a non-qualifying use.

The Value Added Tax (Cars) (Amendment) (No. 1) Order 1992

Also effective from 1 August 1992, this Order allows tax to be reclaimed by persons who let cars on hire to persons who carry on businesses of private taxi firms, self-drive hire firms, and driving schools, but which are not themselves taxable persons.

The Value Added Tax (Increase of Consideration for Fuel) Order 1992

This Order applies to taxable persons from their prescribed accounting periods beginning on or after 6 April 1992, introduces a separate lower scale for taxing diesel fuel, and increases the existing fuel scale for taxing other fuels. The details are as follows:

Private Fuel (3 months)	*Scale rate*	*Petrol Liability @ 17½ %*	*Scale rate*	*Diesel Liability @ 17½ %*
Cars up to 1400cc	£125	£18.62	£115	£17.13
1401 to 2000cc	£158	£23.53	£115	£17.13
over 2000cc	£235	£35.00	£148	£22.04

Note that all these figures are reduced by one-half if business mileage exceeds 4,500 per quarter, and that these figures are reduced by two-thirds in the case of VAT returns submitted monthly.

2.7 SALARY SACRIFICE

The Value Added Tax (Treatment of Transactions) Order 1992

From 1 April 1992, VAT is no longer to be levied in respect of amounts of salary, wages or other emoluments foregone by employees in return for the right to the private use of a motor car provided by their employer (ie salary sacrifice schemes). The Order has no effect in relation to supplies for which the consideration is in a form other than a salary sacrifice.

2.8 PARTIAL EXEMPTION

The Value Added Tax (General) (Amendment) Regulations 1992

With effect from 1 April 1992 (or the first day of the tax year of the registered business if that begins after 1 April 1992), detailed changes are made to the partial exemption rules, broadly in line with some of the proposals made in the 1991 consultation paper, but with certain exceptions.

The main features are:

- A change in the basis for calculating the deductible proportion of non-attributable input tax: this should now be apportioned using the ratio of the value of taxable supplies to all supplies.
- A power for Customs to direct as well as approve the use of alternative methods for apportioning input tax.
- A single de minimis limit of £600 per month on average, in place of the previous three-tier limit.
- An amendment to the list of incidental real estate transactions, whose value is to be excluded from the apportionment calculation.

The new Regulations do not however implement the proposal made in the consultation exercise whereby businesses recover VAT by reference to the previous year's annual adjustment figure, and a further adjustment at the end of the current year. Such a scheme may however be available as a special method, subject to Customs' prior agreement.

2.9 MISCELLANEOUS

Charities
The Value Added Tax (Charities and Aids for Handicapped Persons) Order 1992

Effective from 1 April 1992, this Order allows zero-rating for boats built or substantially adapted for use by the handicapped; extends zero-rating for the provision of toilet facilities for the handicapped to facilities provided in non-residential buildings run by a charity, such as day centres and church or village halls; extends zero-rating to include supplies of repair or maintenance of equipment related to the 'talking books for the blind' scheme run by charities catering for the blind; and extends zero-rating to the provision of spare parts and accessories to those charities providing rescue or assistance at sea.

Registration limits
The Value Added Tax (Increase of Registration Limits) Order 1992

With effect from 11 March 1992 the annual registration limit is increased from £35,000 to £36,600. This represents an increase of around 4.5%, and resumes the practice of increasing the limit roughly in line with inflation – there had been an increase of 37.8% in the previous year. With effect from 1 May 1992, the de-registration limit is increased from £33,600 to £35,100.

Cash accounting
The Value Added Tax (Cash Accounting) (Amendment) Regulations 1992

These Regulations, effective from 1 April 1992, increase to £5,000 the indebtedness a taxable person may have to Customs without being ineligible for admission to the cash accounting scheme – provided there is an arrangement for the outstanding amount to be paid in instalments.

3.1 RATES OF CORPORATION TAX

S.21 The rate of corporation tax for the financial year commencing 1 April 1992 remains unchanged at 33%.

S.22 The rate of corporation tax charged on small companies for the financial year commencing 1 April 1992 remains at 25% and applies where profits do not exceed £250,000. Where a company's profits exceed £250,000, but are less than £1,250,000, the corporation tax charge may be reduced by 1/50 of the difference between £1,250,000 and the company's profits. The effective marginal rate of corporation tax in this band of profits is 35%.

These upper and lower limits are reduced proportionately for accounting periods of less than 12 months and, where there are active associated companies, are divided by one plus the number of associated companies which the company has in the accounting period. Where a company's accounting period spans 1 April, the company's profit is apportioned between the period to 31 March and the period from 1 April for the purpose of applying the above limits.

3.2 GROUP RELIEF

In the Sainsbury case (J Sainsbury v O'Connor), decided in May 1991, it was held that the existence of put and call options did not affect the beneficial ownership of shares before exercise of the options. Nor, in the view of the Courts, did the option facility represent arrangements whereby a shareholder's entitlement to profits on distribution or to assets on a winding up might be changed within the terms of Para 5 (3) Schedule 18 TA and thus potentially affect entitlement to group or consortium relief.

As announced in Parliament in November 1991 and in accordance with draft clauses published in a Press Release in January 1992 the Revenue have legislated to bring the rules into line with what they state to be their previous interpretation of the effect of option arrangements. They have also taken the opportunity to expand and co-ordinate the special rules providing for the calculation of entitlement of an equity holder to distributable profits or to assets in a winding up, where shares have fixed element rights or variable rights. There is no motive test to restrict the application of the new rules to cases where the manipulation of option arrangements is intended.

S. 24 and Sch 6 The schedule inserts even more detailed provisions in place of the previous Para 5 (5) Schedule 18 TA. These identified percentages of deemed distributions of profits or assets in winding up in order to determine share ownership for group relief, etc purposes within the terms of Section 413(7)-(9) in relation to shares with both fixed and variable rights. It is now made clear that the rules apply singly and in combination, to give the lowest possible percentage of profit or asset distribution for purposes of the Section 413 test.

In addition, a new feature is introduced. Where there exist in the accounting period outstanding put or call options, whether in writing or not ('option arrangements'), which would affect percentage entitlement to distributable profits or assets, it is to be assumed that these options have been exercised by purchase of the relevant shares or securities, in all possible combinations of effects, at the point in time when the arrangements come into existence. It does not matter that the rights are not exercisable or capable of being effective at or before the relevant point in time.

At any change in option right there has to be a recalculation of percentage to distributable profits, etc as if the options had been exercised in their different conditions, in order to produce the lowest percentage figure for purposes of qualification for group relief. Nor does it matter if shares or securities were not issued before the option arrangements came into existence.

However, there are certain *restrictions* on the application of the rules for deemed exercise of options as follows:

- Shares do not include fixed-rate preference shares.
- Securities do not include normal commercial loans, as defined in Para 1 (5) Schedule 18.
- Rights to acquire shares do not include rights under an approved employee share option scheme.

There follow very detailed provisions to ensure that, in determining the lowest applicable percentage of profit or asset distribution, all possible combinations of the different features are applied, viz:

- the provisions of Para 4 relating to shares, etc with fixed rights;
- the provisions of Para 5 relating to shares with variable rights;
- the provisions of new Para 5B relating to options; *and*
- the basic provisions of Paras 2 and 3 relating to distribution of profits and assets.

In the most extreme case the lowest percentage resulting from eight possible combinations of provisions would be taken.

Although this cannot readily be ascertained from the wording used, it appears that the Inland Revenue accept that the effect of option arrangements coming into existence may be to 'degroup' a company for group relief purposes from a particular date within an accounting period, but that relief would be available for a notional period up to the date of change. By contrast, surrender of ACT by a parent to a subsidiary company requires grouping of the two throughout the accounting period.

In the case of a combined holding of fixed and variable right shares the relevant event is:

- shares of a relevant company are issued to which both Paras 4 and 5 of Schedule 18 apply; *or*
- shares issued before 15 November begin to carry those rights referred to in Para 4 (1) and those referred to in Para 5(1).

In the case of options the relevant event is when option arrangements are made. Thus existing option arrangements dating before 15 November 1991 should not affect grouping positions.

Particularly in consortium agreements there may be pre-emption rights in the event of one member wishing to sell shares. It is not clear whether a right to buy, contingent on another party wishing to sell, represents an option as defined, but this is expected to be clarified in a statement of practice.

'Option Arrangements' are not defined but it is thought that the Inland Revenue could regard the expression as extending to an understanding between the parties as well as to more formal agreements.

The new provisions apply to accounting periods in which the relevant events occur on or after 15 November 1991.

3.3 COMPANIES CEASING TO BE MEMBERS OF GROUPS

S. 25 Section 25 removes a previous exemption in Sections 178 and 179 TCGA (formerly Section 278 TA 1970) which provide for deemed sales for capital gains purposes of assets previously acquired within a group by the departing company.

Whereas previously a company was held not to have ceased to be a member of a group, and thus not to trigger a gain in respect of a previous internal acquisition, by being wound up or dissolved or in consequence of another member of the group being wound up or dissolved, this exception is only now applicable where a company ceases to be a member of a group in consequence of another member of the group ceasing to exist (ie on the latter being finally liquidated).

The background to the new legislation is that the Revenue did not regard the old provisions as providing exemption where a company left a group on a distribution in the course of a winding up. This interpretation is now applied by law and means that the exemption is of very limited value. Indeed, it is of even more limited value than might appear since Technical Division have stated that in their view the new provisions will apply only to a group consisting of a parent company and a single subsidiary company where the latter ceases to exist, so that the parent ceases to be a member of any group at that time.

Although S178 is an anti-avoidance provision, the exception for companies leaving a group as the result of a winding up, etc did facilitate reorganisations and demergers carried out for good commercial reasons. It is difficult to see the rationale behind the radical changes if these were intended simply to prevent avoidance.

The section applies to a company ceasing to be a member of a group on or after 15 November 1991.

3.4 PROVISION OF DIVIDEND VOUCHERS

S.32 Changes to the requirements to provide vouchers in support of dividend and interest payments have been introduced to ensure that all shareholders receive vouchers and also to align the law with common practice. The vouchers are particularly important to non-taxpayers to enable them to obtain repayment of the tax credit.

For distributions made after Royal Assent, companies are required to provide shareholders or their bank or building society with vouchers in all cases, including where payment is made by electronic transfer. Nominees will also be required to supply vouchers to the beneficial owners of the shares.

Under the previous legislation a dividend or interest payment made by cheque or other order had to be accompanied by a statement or voucher, showing the amount of the payment and the tax credit. However, it is common practice for companies to send a voucher direct to a shareholder and pay the dividend or interest into a bank or building society account. Strictly speaking this did not fulfil the requirements of the legislation since the voucher did not accompany the payment. Provisions have therefore been introduced so that the voucher can be sent separately from the payment.

Failure to comply with the new requirements will result in a penalty becoming payable of £60 per offence, up to a maximum of £600 for any one distribution of dividends or interest.

3.5 DEEP GAIN SECURITIES

S. 33 and Sch 7

The rules relating to the taxation of deep discount and deep gain securities are fairly recent developments and they become more complex as time passes. Once again a schedule adding to the minefield of definitions relating to deep gains has been produced, although it is encouraging that this year the intention is to exclude some securities from the rigours of the deep gain charge which were never originally intended to fall within it.

It has been realised that many bonds which carry a full coupon and were issued at a small discount to par (and thus should not have been within the deep gain rules) are classified as deep gain securities solely because they carry standard event of default or event of risk clauses. The problem arose because the deep gain definition assumes redemption before maturity on the earliest possible happening of an event which might be most unlikely to occur but is nonetheless a term of issue of the security.

The Financial Secretary announced on 12 November 1991 that the 1992 Bill would include legislation providing that securities would not be treated as deep gain securities purely by virtue of a deemed redemption before maturity which might occur by the happening of an event, other than the exercise of a put option, which is prescribed in the terms of issue as one which will or may bring about redemption. He also announced that, by concession, in the meantime the Inland Revenue would not treat securities as deep gain where they fell within the circumstances falling within the contemplated legislation.

Schedule 7 now relaxes the definition of 'redemption' for the purposes of the deep gain test in the following ways:

- For securities issued before 13 November 1991 'redemption' in the context of the test contained in Para 1(2) Sch 11 FA 1989 is not to include any redemption which might be possible before maturity other than:
  - on the exercise of a put option exercisable only on the effluxion of time; *or*
  - the happening of an event which at the time the security was

issued was certain or likely to occur.

These relaxations are introduced by a new Para 1 (3A), Sch 11 FA 1989.

- For securities issued on or after 13 November 1991 the hurdles contained in a new para 1(3B) Sch 11 FA 1989 are greater in number – presumably to avoid terms of issue being drafted with tax specifically in mind. For such securities there is no deemed redemption in cases where the holder does not have a put option if:
  - were there no actual provision for redemption before maturity the interests of the holder might be adversely affected (for example, a default clause);
  - the event occasioning redemption before maturity is neither certain nor likely to occur whether as a single event or as one of a series of events; *and*
  - the obtaining of a tax advantage by any person is not the main benefit, or one of the main benefits, that might accrue from the provision for redemption.

In the case of convertible securities, the second test above is to be treated as fulfilled only with regard to circumstances in which, at the time of issue, the right to convert or exchange cannot be or is unlikely to be exercised.

Furthermore, for securities issued on or after 13 November 1991 a new para 1 (3D), Sch 11, FA 1989 ensures that even the existence of a put option will not imply its exercise if the event allowing the exercise would otherwise have been injurious to the interest of the holder, the event is unlikely to occur and there is no intention to obtain a tax advantage.

Corresponding changes are made in the conditions for classification as a qualifying indexed security which are contained in Para 2, Sch 11, FA 1989 so that, for example, the existence of a default clause does not result in the five-year test failing to be met.

For perpetual bonds (which have no maturity date) the words 'before maturity' are deemed to be omitted from the various tests to ensure they are subject to the same rules.

As an anti-avoidance measure the more liberal provisions relating to default, etc clauses will not apply where there is an actual redemption before maturity and the holder at that time is connected with the issuer. On an actual redemption in these circumstances the security will be treated as having been a deep gain security since its acquisition. Where the security was transferred by a person connected with the issuer within one year of early redemption that transfer will come within the deep gain provisions.

3.6 EUROPEAN COMMUNITY

Transfers of trade
S.44 to S.50 and S.67

These sections contain the major part of the enabling legislation for the EC Mergers Directive. This directive on 'the common system of taxation applicable to mergers, divisions, transfers of assets and exchange of shares concerning companies of different member states' was passed by the Council of Ministers in July 1990. Member states were required to implement the relevant tax reliefs with effect from 1 January 1992.

As the title suggests, the directive provides for tax reliefs and deferrals on a wide range of reorganisations, but in practice the rather precise definitions of the transactions narrow its scope. Further, many of the transactions are not yet possible under the company laws of member states. For instance, a merger requires one company to be dissolved without formal liquidation and to transfer all of its assets and liabilities to a company in another member state. A company law directive and enabling legislation would be required before this becomes generally permissible.

In the light of the company law position, the UK approach to implementation of the tax measures has been to deal only with the transactions that are definitely possible under existing company laws, that is 'exchanges of shares and transfers of assets'. It is quite possible that there are further transactions which could now be implemented which are not within the scope of the new tax provisions.

A 'transfer of assets' is, broadly, the transfer by a company of all of the assets and liabilities of an EC business establishment to a company resident in a different member state, in exchange for securities. The new provisions cover two situations, the transfer of a UK business establishment and the transfer of a foreign branch. In each case the new proposals supplement existing reliefs.

The new reliefs under Sections 44 and 67 apply to transactions on or after 1 January 1992.

Transfer of a
UK trade

An existing relief, Section 172 TCGA (formerly Section 273A TA 1970), deals with the transfer of a trade, carried on in the UK through a branch or agency, to a UK resident company. After the transfer there must be a

75% group relationship between the companies concerned, but the consideration for the transfer can take any form. The effect of the relief is that any assets are treated as sold for a consideration that gives rise to neither gain nor loss to the transferor. In effect this is a limited cross-border extension of the familiar intra-group transfer rules in Section 171 TCGA (formerly Section 273 TA 1970), to cover the incorporation of a UK branch. Section 172 also ensures that the anti-abuse rule in Section 25(3) TCGA 1992 (formerly Section 127(1) FA 1989) does not apply. Otherwise, the transferor would be deemed to dispose of all of its assets at market value, on ceasing to have a UK branch, triggering taxation of the inherent gain on any appreciated assets.

S.44 The new relief on the transfer of a UK trade, Section 140A TCGA, covers a wider range of transactions. The transfer must be between two companies, resident in different member states, one of which may be the UK. There is no minimum common shareholding requirement, but the consideration must be wholly in the form of securities. Such securities may be debt instruments, though it is almost certain that the directive only contemplates consideration in the form of shares.

The effect of the relief is, as in the case of the pre-existing branch incorporation relief, that assets are deemed transferred at a consideration that gives rise to neither gain nor loss. Again, the anti-abuse rule in Section 25(3) does not apply. There is a limitation that gains on the assets transferred must remain within the UK tax net after transfer and not be excluded either by the limited territorial scope of the UK tax law on capital gains or by the effects of a double taxation agreement.

A claim is required for the relief to apply. Benefit is denied if there is no bona fide commercial reason for the transfer or if one of the main purposes of the transaction is to avoid UK tax. There is an optional advance clearance procedure, similar to that for share exchanges under Section 138 TCGA (formerly Section 88). Broadly speaking there is little to choose between the new and the old reliefs.

S.67 This inserts a new Section 152B into the Capital Allowances Act 1990 which provides for continuation treatment for capital allowances purposes.

Transfer of a non-UK trade

In this case there are significant differences between the old relief (Section 140 TCGA, formerly Section 268A TA 1970) and the new, which will be Section 140C TCGA. Both apply, though with different limitations, to transfers of trades carried on outside the UK from a UK company to a non-resident company.

The old relief applies only where, after the transfer, the transferor holds at least 25% of the ordinary share capital of the transferee. The relief is a deferral, possibly indefinite, of the net gain on the transfer, but only to the extent the consideration takes the form of shares or loan stock. The deferred gain is triggered by a sale of the securities or to the extent the transferee sells the transferred assets within six years.

S.45 The new relief takes the form of a notional tax credit rather than a tax deferral. But it is available in a wider range of circumstances, so long as the trade is carried on through an EC branch, the transferee is an EC company and the consideration for the transfer is wholly or partly the issue of securities. There is an anti-abuse rule which denies benefit where there is no bona fide commercial reason for the transfer or UK tax avoidance was one of the main purposes. An optional advance clearance procedure applies, similar to that for share exchanges.

The notional tax credit is provided for under Section 815A TA. The net gain on the transfer is subjected to UK tax but credit is available for tax that would have been paid in the state where the overseas branch business is carried on, but for the effects of the directive. The computation of this credit may well give rise to practical difficulties and if the country where the branch is located already granted tax reliefs before the directive required their introduction, the result could be that no UK tax relief would be available.

To benefit from the new relief, a UK company should attempt to obtain a certificate from the relevant tax authority stating that the gain would have been taxable on the transferor but for the directive and the amount of such tax that would have been payable, computed on the basis that losses and profits arising were aggregated and that all tax reliefs under the foreign law had been claimed.

Following representations, the Inland Revenue accepted that it might not always be possible to obtain an accurate certificate in a reasonable time, so there is an alternative procedure under which the Inland Revenue will compute the notional foreign tax on the basis of information supplied by the taxpayer. This alternative procedure was not contained in the Inland Revenue's consultative paper of December 1991 and is a welcome improvement, as is the extension of the relief to cover cases where the branch is located in the state of residence of the transferee company. Ministers, however, did not heed the suggestion that an extension of the existing Section 140 TCGA would be preferable to the new relief.

Companies will in many cases be able to choose between the two reliefs (they cannot claim both) and this is an issue which will require very careful consideration. Broadly speaking, if a company is confident that there will be sufficient notional tax credit relief to cover tax on the UK measure of the gains, the new relief will preferable, because no deferred gain will be triggered if the securities issued by the transferee company are eventually sold. But in some cases there may be uncertainty as to whether there was a foreign tax relief pre-dating the directive, in which case claiming the old relief might be a more prudent course.

One further difficulty is that there are no special provisions as regards capital allowances. On the face of it the directive would also require a notional tax credit to be available against UK tax on balancing charges, but this is not dealt with in the enabling legislation.

Share exchanges
S.35

This provides for an extension of the tax deferral regime on share for share exchanges. To ensure that the requirement of the Mergers Directive are met, Section 135 TCGA (formerly Section 85 CGTA) will be extended to provide a deferral of tax on capital gains where, as a result of the exchange, the acquiring company holds, or as a consequence of the exchange will hold, the greater part of the voting power of the target company.

The new provision is effective from 1 January 1992. Although introduced to comply with requirements of the EC Mergers Directive, the relief is also applicable to share exchanges involving UK or non-EC companies.

S.36

This is a technical amendment, resulting from the Mergers Directive, to ensure that share for share exchanges do not trigger chargeable events, as regards employee share ownership trusts (ESOPs).

Dividends from EC subsidiaries: paying and collecting agents
S.30

This arises from the EC Parent/Subsidiary Directive, which deals with dividends paid by an EC subsidiary to its parent company in a different member state. One of the requirements of the directive is that there should be no inbound withholding tax. Accordingly, provisions are introduced to ensure that the collecting and paying agent rules of Section 123 TA 1988 do not as of 1 January 1992 require deduction of UK tax where the recipient has a 10% or more voting stake in an EC company paying a dividend.

Transfer pricing
S.51

This contains enabling legislation for the 'Convention on the elimination of double taxation on the adjustment of profits of associated enterprises' introduced as part of the 1990 EC direct tax package, which also contained the Merger Directive and the Parent/Subsidiary Directive. Unlike the directives, the convention requires ratification by all twelve member states before becoming effective. Such ratification is still awaited, so the enabling legislation is currently of little practical consequence.

3.7 INTEREST PAYMENTS

Two new provisions were introduced into the second Finance Bill at Committee stage, following an Inland Revenue defeat at a Special Commissioners hearing.

Perpetual debt
S.31

This extends the meaning of the term 'distribution' for UK tax purposes. It is directed at certain hybrid instruments which might otherwise be classified as debt for UK tax purposes giving an interest deduction to the borrower, but as equity under the rules of the jurisdiction of a foreign lender (although this is not a requirement of the legislation). Were the interest treated as a distribution in the UK it would not be tax deductible and ACT would become payable.

For the new provision to apply the debtor and creditor must be associated by means of a common 75% shareholding, or the debtor must have been 'put in funds' by a company associated in this manner. The form of the lending must be the issue of an 'equity note', ie 'perpetual' debt with either no fixed repayment date or on which the repayment is certain or likely to occur after more than 50 years. It should be noted that some normal intra-group lending arrangements may be at risk if these are informal and there is no clear final date by which repayment of principal must be made.

The provision will not apply if the recipient of the interest is subject to UK corporation tax. In practice, therefore, the provision is discriminatory but because the discrimination is not based solely on the residence status of the recipient, treaty protection is unlikely.

The provision applies to payments made after 14 May 1992, notwithstanding the 'equity note' being already in issue on that date.

Thin capitalisation
S.52

This measure is designed to ensure that the Inland Revenue interpretation of the 'special relationship' provisions in the interest articles of certain tax treaties will prevail in the future. Such treaty provisions provide that where, as a result of a special relationship (such as common control), interest paid by a UK company exceeds what would have been paid in the absence of the relationship, any excess interest is treated in accordance with UK domestic law, without treaty protection. If such interest is paid to a 75% foreign parent, it is then treated for UK tax purposes as a dividend, which is not tax deductible and on which ACT becomes payable.

The new Section 808A TA 1988 provides that, in considering whether there is such excess interest, it is necessary to consider:

- whether the loan would have been made at all in the absence of the special relationship;
- the amount that would have been lent; *and*
- the rate of interest and other terms relating to the loan.

However, the fact that the lender's normal business might not include lending should be disregarded.

The new provision also puts the onus on the borrower to demonstrate that there is no special relationship and the terms that would have prevailed in its absence.

The effect of the new provision, which applies to payments made after 14 May 1992, is to enforce an interpretation of tax treaties which is probably consistent with the negotiators' intentions (at least those on the UK side). Whether this amounts to a treaty override is open to debate.

Some treaties specifically require the question of excess interest to be considered 'having regard to the debt claim for which it is paid'. Where such wording applies, the new statutory interpretation will not prevail and essentially only the rate of interest can be taken into account.

3.8 RENTS PAYABLE BY A CONNECTED PERSON

S.57 A trader paying rent is normally entitled to relief in computing his taxable profits on the amount of rent accruing during the period. The recipient of the rent is, by contrast, chargeable under the Sch A rules on the amount becoming due in the period. Thus the tax treatment of rent paid in arrears could be quite different for payer and recipient and the taxation of the recipient could be deferred without affecting the timing of relief to the payer.

This lack of symmetry is now to be abolished where rent is payable in arrears between connected persons.

A new S33A TA 1988 is inserted which provides that:

- where rents or other receipts chargeable under Sch A accrue in a chargeable period earlier than that in which they are payable,
- the payer is entitled to a deduction in computing his profits or gains, *and*
- the parties are connected when the rents or other receipts accrue, or were connected at any time before they accrue and after both the making of the relevant lease or agreement and 9 March 1992

the recipient will be chargeable under Sch A as the rents, etc accrue rather than as they become payable.

For the purpose of the Sch A charge the rents will be treated precisely as accruing for the purpose of calculating the deduction due to the payer.

The new rules apply to rents accruing from 10 March 1992 and 'connected persons' will be as defined in S839 TA, eg close relatives, companies under common control, etc.

The same basis will apply, by insertion of a new S33B TA 1988, where a third party is interposed between a payer and a connected recipient of rent.

The effect of the change in the rules may be illustrated as follows. Assume that a trading company A Ltd pays rental of £100,000 to its group property company B Ltd on 1 January in arrears for the previous calendar year and that each company has a twelve-month accounting period to 31 December.

- *For the year to 31 December 1991:*
  A Ltd obtains a tax deduction (£100,000) for the rent accruing in 1991.
  B Ltd pays no tax on the 1991 accrual of rent.
- *For the year to 31 December 1992:*
  A Ltd obtains a tax deduction (£100,000) for the rent accruing in 1992.
  B Ltd is taxed on the 1991 accrual of £100,000 to which it became entitled on 1 January 1992 *and* on the rent accruing between 10 March and 31 December 1992 (say £80,500) under the new rule matching taxability with deduction.
- *For the year to 31 December 1993:*
  A Ltd obtains a tax deduction (£100,000) for the rent accruing in 1993.
  B Ltd is taxed on the 1993 accrual of £100,000 and on the rent which accrued between 1 January and 9 March 1992 (say £19,500) to which it became entitled on 1 January 1993.

3.9 CAPITAL ALLOWANCES

Computer software
S.68

In the past, capital sums paid by businesses for software licences may not have qualified for capital allowances; such a licence may not confer title to the software and, in any event, there could be some doubt whether software in fact constitutes machinery or plant.

The CAA is now amended in relation to capital expenditure incurred from 10 March 1992 by a trader in acquiring for the purpose of the trade a right to use or otherwise deal with computer software. In these circumstances, the right and the associated software will be treated as machinery or plant which belongs to the trader so long as he is entitled to the right. Furthermore, where a trader incurs capital expenditure on acquiring computer software outright but the software does not constitute machinery or plant it will be treated as such for capital allowance purposes.

The disposal value to be brought into account under S24 CAA will include capital sums derived from the grant to another person of the right to use or otherwise deal with the whole or part of the software, for example by granting a sub-licence. The amount of the disposal value to be brought into account where the consideration for the right to use software is not wholly an arm's length monetary amount is defined by an addition to the S26 CAA rules.

It should be borne in mind that although capital allowances at 25% on a reducing balance basis are an improvement on the past, a revenue deduction for an increased licence fee (taking the place of the capital sum) will normally be preferable. The rule of thumb is that 'up-front' payments for assets with a useful life of two years or more are capital. If, therefore, a three-year licence is contemplated the licensee might benefit in tax terms by increasing the annual fee rather than pay an ostensible capital sum which would attract only 25% reducing balance allowance.

Enterprise zones
S.70 and Sch 13
Introduction

The concept of enterprise zones was introduced in 1980 in order to encourage businesses to set up in designated areas. Among the incentives available is an initial allowance of 100% (or if the initial allowance is disclaimed a straight line writing down allowance of 25% per annum) for capital expenditure on the construction, extension or improvement of industrial and commercial buildings. In order to qualify for relief the expenditure has to be incurred within ten years of the site first being included in an enterprise zone, or if later, under a contract entered into within that period.

The intention of the original legislation was to allow the relief to the purchaser of an unused building which was acquired after the end of the ten-year period. However, the Inland Revenue were advised that the legislation did not achieve this aim and in order to rectify the position a statement was issued on 16 December 1991 which allowed the relief in the circumstances described on a concessionary basis until the amending legislation came into effect on that date.

Another change is to make it possible for the purchaser of an enterprise zone building to obtain the allowance if it is acquired within two years of it first being brought into use; prior to the date of this relaxation (which applies to buildings first used from 16 December 1991) a purchaser qualified only where the building was bought before coming into use.

Under the previous legislation, expenditure incurred under a contract entered into during the ten-year life of the zone qualified for the allowance no matter when it was actually incurred. A time limit has now been imposed for expenditure incurred from 17 December 1991 (under contracts whenever made) and, in order to qualify, such expenditure must be incurred within ten years of the expiry of the zone, ie within twenty years of the site first being included in the zone.

Finally, the regulations defining an enterprise zone property trust will be amended to give investors allowances where an unused building is bought after the zone expires.

Buildings and structures purchased before use

A new S10A CAA will apply where expenditure has been incurred on the construction of a building or structure not more than ten years after the site was first included in an enterprise zone – or under a contract entered into during that time so long as the expenditure is actually incurred within twenty years of first inclusion in the zone (see new S17A CAA) – and the building or structure is sold without having been used. In these circumstances, the buyer will be deemed to have incurred expenditure equivalent to the lesser of the amount paid for his interest and the actual construction expenditure.

This deemed expenditure is then reduced, for the purposes of the enterprise zone reliefs, where part of the actual expenditure was incurred outside the time limit. In these circumstances, the enterprise zone element is calculated under the formula A x B/C where A is the deemed expenditure, B is the expenditure incurred in the ten-year period (or under a contract entered into during that time and within twenty years of the zone being designated) and C is the actual expenditure whenever incurred.

The non-enterprise zone element (which may for example qualify for the normal industrial buildings allowance) is the difference, if any, between the deemed expenditure and the enterprise zone element.

Where the sale is made by a developer, the price paid by the buyer will constitute his deemed expenditure. In other words, any development profit in the purchase price will qualify for enterprise zone and, where relevant, non-enterprise zone allowances.

Purchases within two years of use

A new S10B CAA is introduced which provides that where qualifying expenditure on a building has been incurred and the relevant interest (as defined in S20 CAA) in that building is first sold within two years of its being brought into use, any balancing allowance or charge on the vendor is to be made in the usual way but the purchaser will be entitled to enterprise zone (and where relevant non-enterprise zone) allowances as if he had incurred expenditure on its construction. The enterprise zone element is calculated in accordance with the formula A x B/C where A is the actual construction expenditure or the price paid by the purchaser whichever is less, B is expenditure incurred (or under a contract entered into) during the ten-year limit and C is the total expenditure. The non-enterprise zone element is the difference, if any, between A and the enterprise zone element.

Where the vendor is the developer the price paid by the purchaser will constitute A in the above formula.

Expensive cars S. 71

The definition of an 'expensive car' for the purpose of restricting capital allowances and tax relief for rental payments was last fixed in 1979 at £8,000. This figure had become increasingly unrealistic and it has now been increased to £12,000 in relation to expenditure incurred or treated as incurred from 11 March 1992, unless it is incurred under a contract entered into before that date. The effect is to increase the maximum writing down allowance to £3,000 per annum and the relief for rental payments is similarly adjusted.

Since it is estimated that 80% of business cars bought or leased in the current year will fall below the new £12,000 limit this figure would appear to be fairly realistic and it is to be hoped that it will be updated more frequently in future.

3.10 UNIFORM BUSINESS RATE

Non-Domestic Rating Act 1992

In his Budget speech Mr Lamont also announced three new measures relating to the Uniform Business Rate (UBR). These deal mainly with adjustments to the transitional provisions that were introduced in 1990, when the UBR replaced the old system of business rates, to ensure that businesses had neither substantial increases nor decreases in their rates bills and provided for such changes to be phased in over a period of years.

The new measures can be summarised as follows:

- where business properties benefit from transitional relief in respect of increases to the UBR bills, the increase for the current year only is to be no more than the rate of inflation;
- from 11 March 1992 transitional relief will no longer be lost on a change of ownership of property;
- business properties subject to the transitional reduction provisions will benefit from increased reductions to that previously specified in their UBR bills in the current year. Furthermore, the transitional provisions are now to be completed by the tax year 1993/94 so that such properties will by that time obtain the full reduction in UBR bills.

These provisions, which have been enacted in the Non-Domestic Rating Act 1992, will lead to a reduction in UBR bills for 650,000 businesses. Local authorities are due to issue adjusted bills in August 1992.

4.1 INCOME TAX: RATES AND ALLOWANCES

Rates and allowances
S.9-10 (FA92)
S.19

The basic and higher rates of income tax remain at 25% and 40% respectively for 1992/93. The threshold at which the higher rate of tax becomes payable remains at £23,700. However from 1992/93 a lower rate of income tax has been introduced such that the first £2,000 of taxable income is liable at 20%.

S.10 (FA92)

Most personal allowances have been increased in line with inflation, the most notable exception being the married couples' allowance which remains frozen at £1,720.

The allowances which will apply for 1992/93 are detailed in Appendix A.

Interest relief
S.10 (FA92)

The limit on qualifying loans (eg for the purchase of private residences) remains at £30,000.

4.2 MARRIED COUPLES' ALLOWANCE: NEW OPTIONS

S. 20, Sch 5 The married couples' allowance is given to the husband and is generally not available to the wife unless the husband's taxable income is sufficient to utilise the allowance.

With effect from the 1993/94 tax year, married couples will be able to allocate the married couples' allowance between them in the following way:

- the wife will be able to elect that she will be entitled to claim one-half of the allowance;
- the married couple may jointly elect that the wife is able to claim the full allowance;
- in a case where the wife is receiving the full allowance, the husband can elect to receive back one-half of the allowance.

If no election is made then the full allowance is given to the husband. If spouses are over the age of 65, higher levels of married couples' allowance can be claimed. However, only an amount up to the basic married couples' allowance can be transferred under these rules.

Elections for sharing the married couples' allowance must be made in the year of marriage or before the tax year in which they are to have effect. The exception is where, in the year before the election is to take effect, the Inspector receives written notification that it is intended to make an election, in which case the election can be made by 5 May in the year of assessment.

The person or persons who make the election can make a withdrawal but that is only effective for the tax year following that in which the notice of withdrawal is received by the Inspector.

There are various provisions enacted to ensure that if either spouse has insufficient income then allocation of the married couples' allowance unutilised is available to the other spouse.

Special rules are introduced in respect of the year of separation and the year of the husband's death for claims for additional personal allowance and widow's bereavement allowance to take account of the sharing of the married couples' allowance.

4.3 CAPITAL GAINS TAX

Rates and allowances
SI 1992/626, S.23

The annual exemption for individuals has been increased to £5,800 for 1992/93. The tax rate on chargeable gains over this amount remains at the individual's marginal rate of income tax, ie 20%, 25% or 40% depending on the level of taxable income.

The annual exemption for most UK resident trusts therefore becomes £2,900.

4.4 GIFTS TO CHARITIES

S.26 The minimum limit for cash gifts by individuals and 'close' companies qualifying for relief under the gift aid scheme as a charge on income is reduced from £600 to £400 (net of basic rate income tax). There is no minimum limit for gifts by 'non-close' companies.

The new reduced limit applies to gifts made on or after 7 May 1992.

S.27 Donations under a charitable deed of covenant qualify for income tax relief if the covenant is capable of running for more than three years. If there is a power of termination that can be exercised outside the minimum period the covenant ceases to be effective when it becomes possible to exercise the power of termination. Usually covenants are then renewed or replaced.

As regards covenants made after 6 May 1992, and existing covenants whose power of termination is exercisable after that date, these covenants will still be treated as tax effective so long as the power of termination is not exercised. It is still necessary for the power of termination to be exercisable only outside the minimum period.

S.28 Certain powers of inspection in respect of books, records and other documents are created to enable the Inland Revenue to process repayment claims made by charitable bodies.

4.5 INTEREST PAYMENTS TO NON-ORDINARILY RESIDENT INDIVIDUALS

S. 29 Previously, non-ordinarily resident persons who made a declaration to that effect so that they could receive interest without deduction of tax had to make a separate declaration to exclude the interest from returns made by the payer to the Revenue.

For interest paid after Royal Assent, a non-ordinarily resident person need only make one declaration both to receive interest gross and be excluded from any returns.

4.6 SPECIAL BENEFITS ON EMPLOYEE SHARES

Definition of special benefits S.37

This section amends Section 80 FA 1988 which imposes a charge to income tax on 'special benefits' received by directors or employees in respect of shares or an interest in shares acquired by reason of their employment.

Special benefits are deemed to be any benefits received by individuals which are not already taxable under the benefits in kind provisions applicable to directors and higher paid employees. These include, for example, the increase in value of shares resulting from the removal of restrictions placed upon them.

In future, regardless of any other relieving provisions, a benefit will be a special benefit for the purpose of S.80 if it is received in respect of shares in a dependent subsidiary with a single class of shares. For this purpose, a company is a dependent subsidiary unless, inter alia, the whole or substantially the whole if its business is carried on with unconnected third parties.

Previously, a benefit was not a special benefit if it was received in respect of *all* shares of the same class. Now it will suffice if the benefit is available to at least 90% of the holders of shares of the same class and, when the payment is received, either:

- the majority of the shares are held otherwise than by or for (i) directors or employees of the company or an associated company, or (ii) the associated company in its own right, *or*
- the company is employee controlled, *or*
- the company is not a dependent subsidiary and the majority of its shares in respect of which the benefit are held otherwise than by or for (i) directors or employees of the company or an associated company or (ii) an associated company which is not the company's parent.

The new provisions apply to benefits received on or after 12 November 1991.

4.7 BUSINESS EXPANSION SCHEME

S.38 BES relief will cease to be available in respect of any shares issued after 31 December 1993.

S.39 The conditions which a company must satisfy in order that its shares qualify for BES relief are relaxed retrospectively to allow companies to have certain property managing subsidiary companies. A 51% subsidiary may exist wholly or substantially wholly for the purpose of holding and/or managing a single block of flats where more than half of those flats are let by the BES company or its subsidiaries in the course of qualifying activities.

S.40 A dwelling house is excluded from the BES where the BES company entered into arrangements for letting it before its acquisition, where it is let at any time on the day of acquisition, or it is let otherwise than on a qualifying long-hold assured tenancy after the company acquires it. Where a property is excluded from the BES this may mean that the company's shares may fail to satisfy the conditions for BES relief.

Those conditions which result in a dwelling house being excluded from the BES are relaxed to allow BES companies to:

(i) enter into letting arrangements with owner occupiers of the property prior to acquisition;
(ii) acquire property already let to the person who was an owner occupier prior to letting and to whom a qualifying tenancy is subsequently granted;
(iii) let a dwelling house on a non-qualifying tenancy provided the letting was to an owner occupier of the property prior to its acquisition and a qualifying tenancy is granted subsequent to the non-qualifying tenancy.

For these purposes 'owner occupier' means a person who:

- at any time prior to the BES company's acquisition, or the letting mentioned in (ii) above of the dwelling house, occupied the dwelling house as their only or principal home and owned a freehold interest in the property; *or*

- for a period of at least two years ending on the date of acquisition by the BES company, or the date of the letting mentioned in (ii) above, occupied the dwelling house as their only or principal home and had an interest in it under a lease for a term of years certain of which not less than 21 years remained unexpired on the date of acquisition or date of letting in (ii) above.

These provisions are intended to facilitate BES involvement in mortgage rescue schemes, although they are of general application where the conditions are satisfied and apply where shares are issued on or after 10 March 1992.

4.8 CAR BENEFITS

SI 1992/731 The scale charges which are used to determine the cash equivalent of the benefit derived from the private use of a company provided car were increased in line with inflation. The scales applicable for 1992/93 are shown in Appendix A.

The Chancellor has announced that a consultative document is to be published concerning car benefit scale charges. The proposal is that whilst the scales will be retained they will in all cases be based on the price of the car rather than engine size.

SI 1992/732 The car fuel scale charges have also been increased in line with inflation by Statutory Instrument, and are shown in Appendix A.

S.53 A new separate scale with a lower tax charge has been introduced for diesel fuel for the year 1992/93, as shown in Appendix A.

4.9 FOREIGN EARNINGS DEDUCTION

S.54 Under Section 193(1) TA, a person who is absent from the UK for a qualifying period of 365 days or more is able to claim a deduction equal to the whole of the earnings attributable to that qualifying period. The legislation which originally introduced this deduction applied to net emoluments after deducting expenses, etc. However, a change made in 1984 had the effect of deleting this restriction with the result that the deduction was then due on gross emoluments.

The Government claims this result was not intended and Section 54, which comes into force with effect from 6 April 1992, reinstates the pre-1984 position. Thus the foreign earnings deduction is given on net earnings after deducting expenses, capital allowances and normal pension contributions.

It is, however, significant that the list of deductions to be made in arriving at net emoluments does not include retirement annuity payments (Section 619) or personal pension plan contributions (Section 639).

4.10 MAINTENANCE PAYMENTS

S.60 Minor technical changes are made to the general rule that subsequent to the Finance Act 1988 no deduction is allowed against taxable income for annuity or annual payments made. Relief is not now given to those claiming a deduction against certain foreign earnings and income from sources in the Republic of Ireland. The change applies from the 1992/93 year of assessment.

S.61 From the 1992/93 year of assessment, relief for maintenance payments will apply to payments made under an order of court or a written agreement in an EC member state, rather than the UK only.

S.62 The present rules governing income tax relief in respect of maintenance payments for the other spouse's maintenance or for the maintenance of a child of the marriage are revised to include maintenance assessed under the Child Support Act 1991 (or Child Support (Northern Ireland) Order 1991). Maintenance assessments will be made by the new Child Support Agency and the change in law ensures that tax relief is given in the same manner irrespective of whether maintenance payments are made under such an assessment or under an EC court order. Since the Finance Act 1988, apart from then existing obligations, income tax relief is limited to the lower of payments made or the married couples' allowance (£1,720 for 1992/93).

Where payments are made under a maintenance assessment in respect of a child of the marriage (including a dissolved or annulled marriage) and the non-payer spouse is a parent of the child, then for the purposes of tax relief the payments will be considered to have been made to the other spouse for the maintenance of that child if collected by the Child Support Agency. Identical treatment is also given where payments are made in respect of income support claimed by the other spouse. Such payments are currently made to the Department of Social Security and will be made to the Child Support Agency in the future. Prior to these changes, tax relief was not available where maintenance was made under a court order in favour of the Department of Social Security, nor would it be available for payments made to the Child Support Agency.

There are transitional rules for persons with existing obligations generally in place before the provisions of the Finance Act 1988 came into force and who have not elected to be treated under the Finance Act 1988 regime. Generally where an existing obligation, eg a pre-1988 court order, is replaced by a maintenance assessment, transitional relief will continue to apply.

These changes will come into force on a future date to be set by statutory instrument, possibly from April 1993.

4.11 FURNISHED ACCOMMODATION

S.58 A minor technical amendment is made to the provisions charging furnished letting income under Case VI rather than Schedule A. The amendment clarifies that a tax charge under Case VI arises where rent is received for the use of premises, irrespective of whether under lease or otherwise. The change applies from 6 April 1992.

'Rent a Room'
S.59 and Sch10

A new relief is introduced to provide a tax incentive for individuals to let out spare rooms in their home. The relief is available, subject to various conditions, to individuals who let furnished accommodation in their only or main residence. The letting income must be taxable under Case I or Case VI of Schedule D, ie trading or furnished lettings, and the relief does not therefore apply to unfurnished lettings.

Where the conditions for relief are satisfied an individual's gross annual receipts from such furnished letting will be exempt from income tax if they do not exceed £3,250. Similarly no capital allowances are available. Where the exemption applies, any letting loss of the year, but not of an earlier year brought forward, is deemed to be nil. In a joint owner situation each owner is allocated one-half of the limit of £3,250 to determine if any exemption is available.

It is important to note that the exemption applies unless an election is made for it not to apply, for example if there is a letting loss. Written elections must be lodged or withdrawn within the 12 months following the end of the year of assessment for which they are to have effect. The Board of Inland Revenue may allow an extension to the election period.

Where gross annual receipts exceed the £3,250 exemption figure the letting income will be taxed on the normal Case I or Case VI basis whichever is appropriate. However, an election can be made for an 'alternative basis' to apply. Under this basis, the difference between the gross annual receipts and the exemption limit (£3,250) is deemed to be letting profit for the purposes of the Case I or Case VI charge. Where a number of sources of gross annual receipt exist the exemption limit is shared on a pro rata basis based on each source's gross annual receipts. Under the alternative basis no capital allowances can be claimed.

The time limits for making an election are 12 months following the year of assessment for which the alternative basis is to apply. An election is automatically withdrawn if gross annual receipts fall below the exemption limit.

Clearly where losses arise in a year of assessment it may be appropriate to claim that the exemption is not to apply in order that these losses are not nullified. As regards the alternative basis this would be advantageous if deductible expenses and capital allowances either do not exceed the exemption limit or they exceed the limit by such a small amount that it is not administratively worthwhile completing a full computation.

Where a married couple take in lodgers it will be necessary to identify who is entitled to the income from letting in order to determine if the exemption limit is available to a spouse or is to be shared.

The ‘rent a room’ provisions apply to income assessable in the 1992/93 and subsequent tax years, even if it arose in a basis period in an earlier tax year.

4.12 INHERITANCE TAX

Increase in zero rate band S. 72

The zero rate band is increased from £140,000 to £150,000 as from 10 March 1992. The rate on chargeable transfers over this amount remains at 20% (lifetime) or 40% (death).

Business property relief S. 73 and Sch14

Certain types of 'business property' qualify for reliefs which reduce their value for inheritance tax purposes. These reliefs are now increased such that assets that qualified for a 50% reduction in value are now fully exempt and those that qualified for the 30% reduction now receive a 50% reduction. The one exception to this change is that controlling shareholdings in fully quoted companies remain eligible only for the 50% reduction.

The definition of unquoted shares has been changed to include Unlisted Securities Market shares (USM), which previously had been treated as quoted shares. Therefore USM shareholdings of up to 25% voting power will now qualify for 50% relief while larger holdings are fully exempt, assuming all other conditions for relief are satisfied.

A corresponding change is made to assets qualifying for agricultural relief, ie the 50% relief is increased to 100% and the 30% relief is raised to 50%.

USM shares and securities will also be considered as 'unquoted' for the purposes of paying inheritance tax by instalments.

These changes apply to events and transfers happening on or after 10 March 1992. The changes to the business property reliefs may also apply to transfers becoming chargeable, or additional tax being calculated, due to the death of the transferor after 9 March 1992 but within seven years of the original transfer, even if the original transfer was prior to 10 March 1992.

5.1 BANKS AND BUILDING SOCIETIES

Certificates of deposit S. 34, Sch 8

The tax rules which apply to certificates of deposit have been extended to cover deposits where there is no actual paper document but there is an entitlement to request one.

All gains on certificates of deposit are treated as income for tax purposes. Interest on most certificates of deposit of over £50,000 can be paid to individuals without deduction of tax.

In practice, most certificates of deposit are lodged with the Central Moneymarkets Office of the Bank of England. These tax changes will enable the Central Moneymarkets Office to make arrangements to handle paperless certificates of deposit which will result in savings in printing and administrative costs.

The new provisions cover arrangements made after Royal Assent.

Paying and collecting agents S. 63, and Sch 11

Changes are being introduced to the way in which paying and collecting agents account for tax they deduct from payments of foreign dividends and interest.

The changes do not affect the circumstances in which agents are required to deduct tax. They are concerned with the payment of tax to the Inland Revenue and are intended both to simplify the system and collect the tax at an earlier date.

At present, paying agents who are appointed by overseas bodies to pay dividends and interest, are required to make a return to the Revenue shortly after a payment is made. However, collecting agents who obtain payment of foreign dividends and interest on behalf of the owners of the income, usually make quarterly returns. An assessment is then raised to recover the tax due, which is payable 30 days after the issue of the assessment.

From 1 October 1992, paying and collecting agents will be required to pay over any tax due to the Revenue within 14 days after the end of the month in which the dividend or interest is paid. Payment of tax will not depend on the issue of an assessment. Interest will be charged from that date on any late payments including those subsequently determined to be due by the Revenue.

Agents will also be required to make quarterly returns of the relevant interest and dividends and the tax thereon, within 30 days of the end of each quarter.

With effect from 1 October, the statutory remuneration received by agents (currently 90p per £1,000 of income from which tax is deducted) will be discontinued.

Retrospective legislation for Composite Rate Tax S.64

Up until 5 April 1991 composite rate tax was payable by building societies and other financial institutions. The tax rate applicable for each year was set by Statutory Instrument.

Following the case won by the Woolwich Equitable Building Society, which found that the provisions for collecting tax for 1986-87 were defective, retrospective legislation was introduced last year to prevent other societies obtaining the same redress. The societies affected are therefore instead seeking judicial review of the validity of the composite tax rates set for the years 1986-87 to 1989-90.

Retrospective legislation has therefore been introduced to remove any doubt that the rates for these years are valid. This is the third, and probably final, attempt at retrospective legislation on the same subject.

Banks and deposit-takers in compulsory liquidation S.66, and Sch 12

Banks and other authorised deposit-takers which are insolvent and in compulsory liquidation will now be able to set off expenses and unrelieved trading losses against interest income received after they have ceased trading, subject to certain conditions.

This relief is intended to increase the amount of money available for distribution to the company's creditors.

Previously, any income arising from a trade which had already ceased was taxable under Schedule D Case VI with relief for expenses and losses incurred prior to cessation. However, some income, such as interest which is specifically taxable under other provisions was taxable without any deductions, despite the fact that in the case of a bank, if still trading, this income would have been treated as trading income.

The new provisions allow banks and deposit-takers to deduct expenses and losses from interest income to the extent they cannot be deducted from other post-cessation income. However, if there is a delay between the cessation of trade and the commencement of winding-up proceedings, expenses incurred in that period will not qualify for the new relief. The new relief applies for chargeable periods ending after 10 March 1992.

5.2 FILM INDUSTRY ALLOWANCES

As announced in the Budget, new reliefs apply to films with sufficient British or other EC qualifying content for which producers have historically been allowed 25% capital allowances on a declining balance basis if they chose to have them certified. Most producers, however, opt for a write-off of costs over the income-producing life of a film or against income on a 'cost recoupment' basis (S.68 CAA).

Relief for preliminary expenditure
S.41

The new reliefs give a full and immediate deduction for 'preliminary' expenditure incurred on or after 10 March 1992:

- with a view to enabling a decision to be taken as to whether or not to make a qualifying film,
- which is not liable to be repaid if the film is not made, *and*
- is payable before the first day of 'principal photography'.

Preliminary expenditure cannot, however, in total exceed 20% of the budgeted total expenditure on the film.

Relief for completed films
S.42

Production expenditure on a completed film is then written off on a straight line basis over three years. Even if a film is completed towards the end of the tax year or accounting period, a full year's one-third write-off is still given for that year. A film is regarded as completed when it is ready for copies of it to be made and distributed for viewing by the general public. This applies to expenditure on a film completed on or after 10 March 1992 even if the expenditure was incurred before that date.

S.69

Both sections require a claim, within two years of the end of the period in which the expenditure under S.41 is payable, and to which the S.42 claim relates, respectively. In the absence of a claim, the previous options for write-off remain open, although it is now specified that the 25% capital allowance basis also requires an irrevocable claim within two years of the end of the period in which the film is completed.

The Inland Revenue have confirmed that expenditure on films acquired, as well as produced, by a taxpayer will qualify. They have also indicated that they will be producing a Statement of Practice to amplify certain aspects of the legislation.

5.3 OIL INDUSTRY

Direct exports of oil and gas
S.55, S.74 and Sch 15

When the Oil Taxation Act 1975 was written, it was a condition of the licence, and one expected to be enforced, that oil and gas be first landed in the UK after production offshore. Accordingly the 1975 oil taxation legislation provided that transportation costs to the UK only are deductible, and specifically excluded a deduction for transportation costs for oil and gas taken somewhere other than the UK.

This situation became unsatisfactory once oil fields were developed where oil was loaded into tankers offshore, rather than being fed into a pipeline system which took the oil directly to the UK. Where tanker loading was the means of shipping oil from the field, it was often the case that the owner of the oil wished to use the tanker to transport the oil directly to a customer, say in The Netherlands or Germany. The licence condition that the oil be first landed in the UK was waived in these circumstances.

Extra-Statutory Concession I2 was introduced to solve the tax deductibility problem, so that, by concession, where oil is directly exported to a country other than the UK from a field by tanker, the cost of transportation to the actual point of delivery is allowed, up to the amount which would have been the transportation costs if the oil had actually been landed in the UK.

The Extra-Statutory Concession applies only to tanker-loaded oil. Recently, however, there has been considerable interest in exporting gas directly from the UK sector through pipelines which will take the gas directly from the field either to The Netherlands or to Germany. It was considered by Ministers that the allowance of such transportation costs would require legislation rather than extension of the Extra-Statutory Concession.

The provisions in the Finance Act ensure that a deduction for the transportation costs of oil and gas produced offshore and taken to the nearest reasonable point of landing outside the UK is available for Petroleum Revenue Tax and that for Corporation Tax purposes the deductions related to such transportation fall within the ring fence rather than outside it. The provisions also apply to tanker-loaded oil, so that Extra-Statutory Concession I2 is no longer required.

5.4 FRIENDLY SOCIETIES

S.56 and Sch 9 Under the new Friendly Societies Act 1992, friendly societies will be able to incorporate and thus be able, through subsidiaries, to provide a wider range of financial services such as the running of PEP schemes. Without further special provisions the effect of incorporation on the tax position of a registered friendly society writing tax-exempt or partly exempt business and the position of its members could be adverse in various ways. The provisions detailed below avoid these difficulties and make consequential amendments to the existing legislation relating to friendly societies and their members.

The existing treatment of registered friendly societies is extended to incorporated societies, as follows:

- The treatment of policyholders in relation to premiums and gains on qualifying policies.
- Inclusion of an incorporated society in the list of qualifying lenders for MIRAS purposes.
- Exemption from income tax and corporation tax for registered friendly societies in respect of life or endowment business in relation to small contracts, but subject to existing limitations applying to non-incorporated societies.
- The provisions which allow carry forward of management expenses and losses on the transfer of all or part of the long-term business of one insurance company to another which ensure that there is no disposal for capital allowances purposes solely because of the transfer. These provisions are extended to incorporated friendly societies and therefore to the act of incorporation by a society.
- Similarly there is to be no gain/no loss disposal for capital gains purposes on incorporation.

There are also provisions for continuity of relief to incorporated societies formed by the amalgamation of two or more friendly societies.

There is one further new provision – income from a subsidiary company not referable to the parent's tax exempt life or endowment business is not to be exempt.

5.5 LIFE ASSURANCE BUSINESS: I-E BASIS

S.65 Although life assurance companies are trading companies and may have all their income assessed under Case I of Schedule D as trading income, in practice life companies have been assessed under the other cases of Schedule D on the so-called income less expenses (I - E) basis. The I - E basis also allows the Revenue to assess the policyholders' investment income irrespective of the size of the company's own surplus. When however, a Case I loss is made, and a company claims to relieve this by set-off against other income or by surrender as group relief to another company in the same group, the Inland Revenue may seek to put limitations on the extent to which relief is achieved.

It has recently been suggested that the Inland Revenue cannot exercise its option to tax on the I - E basis where the company has claimed relief for a Case I loss. This would have adverse consequences for the Revenue in some instances but also for life companies which had excess expenses on the I - E basis which might technically be prevented from being carried forward. A second argument might be advanced to prevent the Revenue applying the I - E basis. This is that a number of provisions specific to life assurance taxation require investment income from assets of the long-term fund to be included in a computation of profit from that business. It has been suggested that these provisions might require the income to be so taxed under Case I.

It is for these reasons, it seems, that new provisions have been introduced to ensure that the I - E basis is not prevented from applying to a company's life assurance business, including its annuity business, and also that the calculation of income and gains of the life business is not affected by any of the following:

- the making of a relevant claim in respect of trading losses. A relevant claim for this purpose is one involving trading losses carried forward or back, set off sideways or surrendered as group or consortium relief,
- the application of any commercial or accounting principle or practice in computing a trading loss, *or*

- the application of provisions governing the basis for inclusion of investment income in a Case I-style computation of a life company.

The legislation is deemed always to have applied to past periods. This element of retrospection will no doubt be justified by the Inland Revenue on the grounds that the legislation merely confirms what was always thought to be the position. However, if the legal position was uncertain, it must be debatable whether such an approach can be justified.

5.6 NORTHERN IRELAND ELECTRICITY (NIE)

S. 77, Sch 17 Schedule 17 incorporates measures to facilitate the vesting of assets under a transfer scheme laid down by the Electricity (Northern Ireland) Order 1992. It will apply to transfers from NIE to successor companies, and to any subsequent transfer to further successor companies.

In particular, it provides for the following:

- the successor companies will be treated as if they had always carried on the transferred trade and a proportion of NIE's unallowed tax losses (both trading and capital) and capital expenditure eligible for capital allowances will be apportioned to each successor company. Any dispute on apportionment shall be determined by the General Commissioners and, in special circumstances, by the Special Commissioners;
- for purposes of roll over relief, the successor companies will be treated as if they had owned the assets and used them in the same manner as NIE;
- all interest paid on securities issued under the Electricity (Northern Ireland) Order 1992 will be deductible for corporation tax purposes even though the interest may be expressed as for a period before the security was actually issued;
- any agreement made for the purpose of or for purposes connected with the transfer scheme will be outside of the charge to stamp duty reserve tax.

6.1 GENERAL AND SPECIAL COMMISSIONERS

S. 75, S. 76 and Sch16

In November 1991 the Lord Chancellor's department and the Inland Revenue published a consultative document which addressed a number of issues concerning General and Special Commissioners, including:

- The possibility of a change of name which would more accurately reflect the functions of both sets of Commissioners.
- The reporting of decisions of Special Commissioners.
- The award of costs by Special Commissioners in certain circumstances.

The document also contained draft procedural rules (based largely on the model rules of procedure set out by the Council on Tribunals) which included significant changes to the informal systems at present in operation.

S.75 provides that the Lord Chancellor may, with the consent of the Lord Advocate, make regulations for both categories of Commissioners to hold office by different (as yet unspecified) names.

Sch 16 amends the TMA as follows:

- From April 1994 the Lord Chancellor (or the Secretary of State for Scotland) are responsible for paying the expenses of General Commissioners and the remuneration of their clerks.
- The Lord Chancellor may with the consent of the Lord Advocate make regulations giving greater flexibility to both categories of Commissioners to determine jurisdiction in relation to appeals and other proceedings.
- The Lord Chancellor, with the consent of the Lord Advocate, is also given power to make regulations regarding the procedures in connection with appeals, including:
  - the joining of parties to appeals,
  - the power to require from the parties the production of information and documents,
  - the power to require persons to attend, give evidence and produce documents,

- provisions as to evidence generally,
- provisions to enable Commissioners to review their decisions (for example, where a party had good reason to fail to appear or to adduce relevant evidence),
- power to impose and recover penalties,
- procedures for stating cases for the opinion of a court,
- the award, only by Special Commissioners, of the costs of hearings before them; costs will be awarded only where either party had acted wholly unreasonably in contesting an appeal,
- the publishing by the Special Commissioners of reports of such of their decisions as they consider appropriate; the consultative document proposed that the Presiding Special Commissioner should select decisions for reporting in anonymised form.

The Chancellor said in his Budget speech that the new procedural rules would come into effect in April 1993. When the appropriate regulations are published it will be possible to judge whether representations made as a result of the consultative process (for example that it should be possible to apply for a summons to produce documents to be set aside) have been successful.

A RATES AND ALLOWANCES 1992-93

Income Tax

Taxable income Bands	*Rate*	*Tax on Band*
£	%	£
0-2,000	20	400
2,001-23,700	25	5,425
Excess	40	

Allowances	£
Persons under age 65	
Personal allowance	3,445
Married couples' allowance	1,720
Persons aged 65 to 74	
Personal allowance	4,200
Married couples' allowance	2,465
Persons aged 75 and over	
Personal allowance	4,370
Married couples' allowance	2,505
Income limit for age allowance	14,200
Additional relief for single parent	1,720
Widow's bereavement	1,720
Blind person	1,080
Mortgage interest loan limit	30,000

Capital gains tax

Gains are taxed at the individual's marginal income tax rate, or in the case of discretionary trusts at 35%.

Annual exemptions	£
Individuals, personal representatives and trusts for disabled people	5,800
Other trust	2,900

Inheritance tax

Chargeable values from 10 March 1992 from	*On death*
£	*Rate %*
0 – 150,000	Nil
Excess	40

Transfers made within seven years of death are liable at the death rate subject to tapering relief on transfers between seven years and three years before death as follows:

Charge on gifts within seven years of death:

Intervening years	*0-3*	*3-4*	*4-5*	*5-6*	*6-7*
% of full charge	100	80	60	40	20

Chargeable lifetime transfers which are not potentially exempt transfers are charged at half the full rate but additional tax may become payable by reference to the full rate if the transferor dies within seven years of making the gift.

Exemptions	£
Annual gifts per donor	3,000
Small gifts per donee	250
For marriage, from	
parents	5,000
grandparents, etc	2,500
parties to the marriage to each other	2,500
others	1,000

Car and fuel benefits

	Car Benefit		Fuel Benefit	
	Under four years old	*Four years old or more*	*Petrol*	*Diesel*
	£	*£*	*£*	*£*
Car costing up to £19,250				
1400cc or less	2,140	1,460	500	460
1401 – 2000cc	2,770	1,880	630	460
over 2000cc	4,440	2,980	940	590
Cars costing from £19,251 to £29,000	5,750	3,870	*	*
Cars costing over £29,000	9,300	6,170	*	*

- Car and fuel scales are reduced by 50% if business mileage is 18,000 miles or more in the year.
- Car scale is increased by 50% for a second car or if business mileage in a tax year is less than 2,500.
- Car scale is reduced pound for pound for contributions an employee is required to make for private use.
- Fuel scale is reduced to nil if the employee makes good all the fuel for private journeys.

*Depends on engine size, as with cars costing up to £19,250.

Pension contribution limits

Personal pension schemes		*Retirement annuity schemes*	
Age on 6 April	*% NRE + **	*Age on 6 April*	*% of NRE +*
35 or less	17.5		
36 – 45	20.0		
46 – 50	25.0	50 or less	17.5
51 – 55	30.0	51 – 55	20.0
56 – 60	35.0	56 – 60	22.5
61 or over	40.0	61 or over	27.5

+ Net relevant earnings

* Subject to a maximum of £75,000 of earnings

B ERNST & YOUNG OFFICES IN THE UK

Aberdeen	50 Huntly Street, Aberdeen AB9 1XN, Tel: 0224 640033
Belfast	Bedford House, 16 Bedford Street, Belfast BT2 7DT, Tel: 0232 246525
Birmingham	PO Box 1, 3 Colmore Row, Birmingham B3 2DB, Tel: 021-626 6262
Bristol	One Bridewell Street, Bristol BS1 2AA, Tel: 0272 290808
Cambridge	Compass House, 80 Newmarket Road, Cambridge CB5 8DZ, Tel: 0223 461200
Cardiff	Southgate House, Wood Street, Cardiff CF1 1EW, Tel: 0222 645444
Dundee	Ten Constitution Road, Dundee DD1 9PN, Tel: 0382 313131
Edinburgh	17 Abercromby Place, Edinburgh EH3 6LT, Tel: 031-556 8641
Exeter	Broadwalk House, Southernhay West, Exeter EX1 1LF, Tel: 0392 433541
Glasgow	George House, 50 George Square, Glasgow G2 1RR, Tel: 041-552 3456
Hull	PO Box 3, Lowgate House, Lowgate, Hull HU1 1JJ, Tel: 0482 25531
Inverness	Moray House, 16 Bank Street, Inverness IV1 1QY, Tel: 0463 237581
Ipswich	Queens House, Queen Street, Ipswich IP1 1SW, Tel: 0473 217491
Leeds	PO Box 61, Cloth Hall Court, 14 King Street, Leeds LS1 2JN, Tel: 0532 431221
Leicester	Provincial House, 37 New Walk, Leicester LE1 6TU, Tel: 0533 549818
Liverpool	Silkhouse Court, Tithebarn Street, Liverpool L2 2LE, Tel: 051-236 8214
London	Becket House, 1 Lambeth Palace Road, London SE1 7EU, Tel: 071-928 2000
Luton	400 Capability Green, Luton LU1 3LU, Tel: 0582 400700
Manchester	Commercial Union House, Albert Square, Manchester M2 6LP, Tel: 061-953 9000
Newcastle upon Tyne	Norham House, 12 New Bridge Street West, Newcastle upon Tyne NE1 8AD, Tel: 091-261 1063
Norwich	Cambridge House, 26 Tombland, Norwich NR3 1RH, Tel: 0603 660482
Nottingham	10-12 The Ropewalk, Nottingham NG1 5DT, Tel: 0602 411861
Peterborough	New Priestgate House, 57 Priestgate, Peterborough PE1 1JX, Tel: 0733 60348
Reading	Apex Plaza, Reading RG1 1YE, Tel: 0734 500611
Sheffield	Talbot Chambers, 2-6 North Church Street, Sheffield S1 2DH, Tel: 0742 752929
Southampton	Wessex House, 19 Threefield Lane, Southampton SO1 1TW, Tel: 0703 230230
Swindon	Old Town Court, 10-14 High Street, Swindon SN1 3EP, Tel: 0793 618822